Worshiper by Design:

A Unique Look At Why We Were Created

John W. Stevenson

*Worshiper by Design: A Unique Look At Why
We Were Created*
by John W. Stevenson

Printed in the United States of America

ISBN 9781615791637

Unless otherwise indicated, Bible quotations are taken from

> The NEW AMERICAN STANDARD BIBLE. Copyright © 1960, 1962, 1963, 1968, 1971, 1972, 1973, 1975, 1977 by The Lockman Foundation. Used by permission.
> THE NEW KING JAMES VERSION (NKJV). Copyright © 1982, by Thomas Nelson, Inc.
> The HOLY BIBLE, NEW INTERNATIONAL VERSION (NIV) ®. Copyright © 1973, 1978, 1984 by International Bible Society. Used by permission of Zondervan Publishing House.
> THE MESSAGE: The Bible in Contemporary Language. Copyright © 2002 by Eugene H. Peterson.

www.xulonpress.com

Endorsements

For many years, my spiritual father Apostle John W. Stevenson has poured nuggets of truth and wisdom into me regarding the subject of true worship. Now, any and everyone (bar none) who reads this book will benefit from the amazing revelations God has given him. This book put brakes on my endless pursuit of "doing" worship, and sets me on a path of "being" the worshiper God created me to BE!
Darwin Hobbs, Gospel Recording Artist

I'm always intrigued to hear from pastors who also have a passion and depth of understanding of worship. JWS is one of those people and one of my favorites. A lot of your favorite worship leaders and artists are appreciated by you because of John's input and insight regarding worship in their lives. My life is one of those. This book can both encourage and challenge you. I pray that you allow it to do both.
Israel Houghton, Grammy Award-winning Singer, Songwriter, Producer and Recording Artist

We live in a time in history where more information about worship is available than ever before. However, there are many echoes of the same prevailing thought. Through the sea of voices, there are a few who speak the truth with authority because their writing is not just an idea passed down to them from another, but a God thought shaped through a lifestyle of intimacy with God and obedience. Pastor John W. Stevenson is a voice shaped by the lifestyle of worship and obedience to God. As a result a fresh perspective on an often-written about subject is released and is a must read for all who seek to know intimacy with God in a new way. Worshipers, (that is everyone, not just those in the arts) you need to read this book!

William McDowell, Recording Artist and Worship Pastor of The Gathering Place Worship Center, Lake Mary, Florida

If you, as a Kingdom Worshiper, had to possess one relevant book besides your Bible that would give your life balance and lead you to the authentic, true meaning of worship – this would be it. This book is life-changing. Apostle John W. Stevenson has taken us back to God's precise purpose for true worship. This book should be a major staple in the library of every child of God. Apostle teaches us what we have gotten away from where true worship is concerned. The writings of Apostle John have changed my "worship life" forever.

Min. John Murray II, Worship Leader/Assistant Minister of Music, Potter's House Of Dallas, Inc.

I love books that challenge me and cause me to search the Word of God even more. This book will do just that. The first few lines of the book gave me a real jolt because of something I have been taught and sung about most of my life. It is my prayer that John's book will help restore us back to real intimacy with our Creator and, thus, we will become more productive.
Morris Chapman, Songwriter & Recording Artist

The pen that has written prophetic songs has now given us a prophetic book that cuts pass our typical assumptions about worship and releases the purity of a true heart song. Worship your way through this provocative read.
Bob Sorge, Author and Founder of Oasis House Ministries

This book is designed to align your heart with God's heart on the subject of worship. John W. Stevenson is a dear friend who has pursued God's Presence in both corporate and private setting for many years. I encourage you to take a fresh and inti-mate journey into the meaning of worship, and the call of the worshiper
Clarence Grant, Minister of Music, Covenant Church of Pittsburgh

To take a journey to a familiar place where you know all the shortcuts and back roads, only to find that some of the roads are over grown with weeds can be disconcerting. We then find that another path must be taken in order to arrive at our familiar destination. John takes us on a familiar journey with freshness and boldness to thrust us into a position of reexamining our views and teachings on this very familiar subject. This book helps us "rightly divide the word of truth" regarding worship.

Valerie R. Harris, Levitical Vessels, Inc.

It is an honor for me to recommend Apostle-Pastor John W. Stevenson's book, *Worshiper by Design: A Unique Look at Why We Were Created.* From the challenge in Chapter One to assess our motivation for worship through to a call back to authentic, passionate worship in subsequent chapters, this book encompasses a relevant, vital message for the Body of Christ and is a valuable resource for every worshiper.

Vivien Hibbert, President and Academic Dean of the Worship Arts Conservatory

Apostle John W. Stevenson has captured the heart of God in describing His creative purpose for humanity. He adjusts our theology to reflect who we are created to *"be," worshipers who have Kingdom Dominion.* In his book we discover that true worship is a lifestyle that responds in obedience to the will of God. A must read for every believer.

Pastors Harold & Fellicia Duncan, Abundant Life Christian Center, Redford, MI

Finally, the fresh, authentic truth about worship that my generation has been craving! This book will

revolutionize your life as a worshiper as it clearly answers questions about this subject that have often been misunderstood in the Body of Christ.
Arnez Booker, Founder and President of the ELITE Program

John W. Stevenson's new book is a teaching that is so critical to the Body of Christ. It brings freedom to every believer to understand they are worshipers in every aspect of their lives, no matter what vocation God has called them to. This book brings revelation and freedom to all believers (especially those of us who don't sing very well or play an instrument) to "be" who God created them to "be" as they do what God created them to do. I thank God for the revelation that He has poured into John and John's courage to put it in this teaching.
Ford Taylor, Co-founder of Transformation Cincinnati/Northern Kentucky

Dedication

I dedicate this book, first and foremost, to my children, grandchildren and to the future generations of worshipers. May the reading of this book help you to know the true essence of why you were created and help you to truly become the worshipers you were created to be!

Secondly, I dedicate this book to every believer who has ever been made to feel that you were not a worshiper because you did not sing, dance or play a musical instrument! Now you know the truth! You are a worshiper by design!

Lastly, I dedicate this book to you the reader who holds this book in your hands!

Table of Contents

Foreword

One of my mentors taught me *"All progress in the Christian life is by faith."* I have had more than thirty years to examine by experience the profound simplicity of those words and I have concluded that he is absolutely correct. Hosea says, "Then shall we know if we follow on to know the Lord" (Hosea 6:3 KJV). Faith is a by-product of a relationship with God; "He is a rewarder of those who seek Him" (Hebrews 11:6b *NASB95*). Every biblical example of the true worshiper demonstrates a pattern of one who is seeking a relationship with God. On three different occasions in the scriptures, Abraham is called "a friend of God." God didn't create Adam because He needed a gardener; He wanted intimacy from a son.

When Abraham began to pursue God in his wanderings, in each place he moved, he had two priorities: to pitch a tent and build and altar. If altar building for the purpose of sacrifice becomes natural to us, we can do it under the extreme pressure of offering your son upon one. Abraham knew how to build an altar and he knew it was for sacrificing life.

The accoutrements of worship are often confused for the actual worship, and so we spend more time embellishing the "scaffolding" (music, ambience, singers, etc.) that enable us to "build" a portion of the atmosphere that will eventually produce true worship.

Samuel rebuked Saul because he thought that sacrifice was more important than doing what God had commanded him to do. If I were to paraphrase Samuel's words to Saul, he essentially declared, "Obedience is the highest form of worship." What if the Lead Worshiper, began the service of worship by saying, "Let us obey God!" Not let us turn to hymn number whatever… John Stevenson is a mature pastor, whose experience in the ministry of music, writing, teaching and leading people into the presence of God is rich in its broad embrace of a multitude of genre. He is not a novice and deserves to be heard in what it means to be a true worshiper. John could wear without pretension the "Been there – done that!" t-shirt.

What you will encounter in this book is a spiritual father's appeal to persons who are just getting started and to those of us who have been on the journey for a while to reexamine what we are seeking to impart and teach to a multitude of people who are being awakened to this new season of interest in worship as a lifestyle. I encourage you to read it with an open mind and heart and hearing what the Spirit might be saying to us.

Bishop Joseph L. Garlington, Sr.
Senior Pastor
Covenant Church of Pittsburgh

Acknowledgements

First and foremost, I want to thank the Lord for saving me, blessing me and keeping me. I thank Him for the wonderful privilege of serving Him and serving the people God. I am humbled and eternally grateful.

To my wife Marissa, you are the love of my life, my companion for life. Thank you for sharing your life with me and sharing me with the world. I could not do this without you. Thank you for being patient with me each time I enter into a project that takes me away from you. Your sacrifice has not gone unnoticed and will not go unrewarded. I love you.

To my children: my son, John G. and his wife, Juaacklyn, my daughter Leslie, my sons, Nicholas, David, Christopher, and my first grandson, Bishop, I love each of you beyond measure. It remains my joy to see each of you grow in your relationship with the Lord. I pray that you continue to walk out the purpose and destiny that God has for each one of you! I love you.

To my mother, Patricia Stevenson, thank you for your love and support of me and my ministry over the years. To my siblings, Ray, Brett (Barbi), Edith (Virgil), and Larry (Joy), there is nothing more important than family. I love each of you very much. To my wonderful in-laws Paul and Ernestine Menefield, (Stevie and Kevin, too) thank you for your love and support also!

To the Heirs International Ministries team, thank you for your support in helping me to take this ministry to the nations! To my friends, Eddie and Vanessa Luckey, you are a great team to work with. Thanks for keeping me organized and focused. To my son, Nicholas Stevenson, your gift has already made room for you. Welcome to the team! Let's get busy!

To the members and leadership team of Heirs Covenant Church of Cincinnati, thank you for allowing me the honor to serve as your pastor. You are a great church and a great body of worshipers. I love you all very much!

To Bishop Joseph and Pastor Barbara Garlington, I could not ask for better pastors. You are both incredible gifts to the Body of Christ, and I am grateful to the Lord to have you as a covering. Thank you for loving me, supporting me, and sharing your world with me.

To my friend and my editor, Deborah A. Gaston, you are a gift from God! Thank you for all of the time and effort you put into this book. Thank you for the editing, rewrites, and additions that helped to make this message clear. Thank you for gently pushing me to write a good book! You are a blessing to me and a true worshiper!

To John and Susan Perodeau and all of those who have helped in any way to make this project a reality, I say "Thank You" and to God be the glory!

INTRODUCTION

HELP! MY PASTOR IS NOT A WORSHIPER!

I can't tell you how many times I have been teaching at a conference or have been invited to a church to teach a seminar on worship when some well-meaning attendee or member of the church comes up to me "in private" (kind of like Nicodemus coming to Jesus) and says, "I am so glad the Lord brought you here. We need this kind of teaching." Then they will make this statement: *"My pastor is not a worshiper!"*

I first ask them, "How do you know he is not a worshiper? What gauge or standard are you using to come to that conclusion?" They usually respond by saying, "The pastor never raises his hands during the worship," or "He never sings the songs," or "He always cuts the worship time short." At that point I usually ask them to tell me about their church and the pastor. I encourage them not to be so critical or judgmental of the pastor, and I urge them to talk with their pastor and to be open to his perspective. I walk away thinking how unfair they are to make that kind of judgment.

I believe that this kind of thinking stems from what has been traditionally taught about worship and the worship life of the believer! We only know what we have been taught. Unfortunately, some of what we have been taught is not accurate. It has led to misinformation, and misinformation will always lead to wrong interpretation and application. We have taught on worship in a way that has made it synonymous with music and the arts. For that very reason, many who have musical or artistic gifts feel that if others do not have a musical or artistic expression in their worship, they are not true worshipers. We have focused on the worship team, the praise dancers, the banners and flags, the choir and the musicians. We have focused on our music departments. All of these areas of ministry are good and provide us with wonderful vehicles for worship. Lamentably, because of the emphasis we have placed on music, dance and other artistic forms, we have deemed those who participate in these areas *the* worshipers, and everyone else can be made to feel as if they are mere "church members." We have done a great disservice to the Body of Christ through some of the things we have taught concerning worship and what it means to be a true worshiper.

I absolutely believe that music is a gift from God to enhance the worship life of the church. I believe that music is a spiritual language that allows us to communicate thoughts and feelings in ways in which words often times fall woefully short. It has only been in recent years that I have felt a caution in my spirit as it relates to some of the things I, as well as others, have taught over the years about worship. Because of conversations like the one with the disgruntled "worshiper," I began feeling that something was not quite right in our teachings. That led me to seek the Lord for answers. As a result, I have realized that much of what I have heard taught, and even much of what I myself have taught has led us down a path that has made the worshiper a member of an exclusive group of gifted singers, musicians, dancers and those artistically gifted. We have focused more on the use of the gifts than the lifestyle. We have taught a perspective that has unintentionally created a caste system, a tier system, an "us-and-them" system. It is a system that, if not addressed and changed, could leave many believers feeling like second-class citizens in the Kingdom of God, while others, because of their gifting, may feel as if they are the "chosen" ones.

I believe that God wants to level the playing field in His Church. In order for that to happen, we must re-examine what we have taught and we must be willing to make whatever adjustments necessary to bring balance to our message. We now must be willing to look at the models we have used for worship, to look at the vocabulary we have used, and find a different approach to our teaching on worship — one that is more inclusive of all the members of the Body of Christ. It is my conviction that we must do all we can to help the Body of Christ return to a more biblically accurate perspective on what it means to be a worshiper. In order to accomplish this, it's important for us to ask ourselves some questions:

- What was God's original intention for man?
- What did God mean when He said *"Let Us make man in Our own image?"*
- Is it true that we were created to worship God?
- What does it really take to be a worshiper?
- Is there a biblical definition of a worshiper?
- If worship of God is really exemplified through singing, playing instruments, dancing and other expressions associated with the arts, why doesn't everyone have at least one of those gifts?
- Where did our focus and emphasis on music and the arts in worship come from?
- From where and from whom should we draw our worship model?

I believe as we explore these and other questions, you will see that there is more to consider about worship and the worship life of the believer.

It is my prayer that as you read this book, the Lord will give you eyes to see, ears to hear, and an open heart and mind to receive its contents. It is my prayer that as you read this book, your heart will be stirred with new passion to pursue Him in a fresh way! It is my prayer that by the completion of this book, you will have a new perspective, a new way of thinking about worship and the worship life of the church that you will carry for the rest of your life.

CHAPTER ONE

Created To Worship?

*W*e were not created to worship God! This statement may seem like heresy, but it's not. Do I
believe we should worship God? Absolutely! He is
worthy of all worship! I am not saying we should
not worship God, but I am addressing a statement we
have made for many years without taking the time to
fully consider what we are saying. I submit to you
again: we were not created *to* worship God! In order
to understand this statement, we need to look at the
Scriptures and revisit God's original intent for man.
God is intentional and specific about everything He
says and everything He does! With God nothing is by
chance; nothing is left to chance. Let's go back to the
beginning and look at all that God created, how He
created it, and what He said when He created it all.

Let There Be...

The first chapter of Genesis is familiar to all of us; it is the account of the creation. As we read, we can note a pattern that will help us better understand that our created purpose is not *to* worship God. The first command that God gave is seen in verse 3. God simply spoke, "Let there *be* light...!"

> *"Then God said, **"Let there be light;"** and there was light. And God saw that the light was good; and God separated the light from the darkness. And God called the light day, and the darkness He called night. And there was evening and there was morning, one day."* (Genesis 1:3-5 emphasis added)

As we continue to read, we find these words: "Let there *be* an expanse. . ."

> *"Then God said, **"Let there be an expanse in the midst of the waters**, and let it separate the waters from the waters." And God made the expanse, and separated the waters which were below the expanse from the waters which were above the expanse; and it was so. And God called the expanse heaven. And there was evening and there was morning, a second day."* (Genesis 1:6-8 emphasis added)

He then said, "Let there *be* lights in the expanse of the heaven..."

*"Then God said, **"Let there be lights** in the expanse of the heavens to separate the day from the night, and let them be for signs and for seasons and for days and years; and let them be for lights in the expanse of the heavens to give light on the earth"; and it was so. God made the two great lights, the greater light to govern the day, and the lesser light to govern the night; He made the stars also. God placed them in the expanse of the heavens to give light on the earth, and to govern the day and the night, and to separate the light from the darkness; and God saw that it was good. There was evening and there was morning, a fourth day."* (Genesis 1:14-19 emphasis added)

Can you see the pattern? In each instance God said, "Let there *be...*" In essence, He was saying, "Light, be! Expanse, be! Lights, be!" And the moment He spoke, it came into being! God first said, "Be!" and then He declared what that state of being would bring about.

It is in Genesis 1:26 that we read of the creation of man. God began by making this declaration, *"Let Us make man in Our own image, in Our own likeness."*

*Then God said, **"Let Us make man in Our image, according to Our likeness;** and let them rule over the fish of the sea and over the birds of the sky and over the cattle and over all the earth, and over every creeping thing* *that creeps on the earth." And God created man in His own image, in the image of God He created him; male and female He created them. And God blessed them; and God said to them, "Be fruitful and multiply, and fill the earth, and subdue it; and rule over the fish of the sea and over the birds of the sky, and over every living thing that moves on the earth."* (Genesis 1:26-28 emphasis added)

Man was created to *be* the reflection of God in the earth; the reason for his existence was to *be* a mirror image of God. Man was created to *be* like God and to rule and reign as lord of the earth as God rules and reigns as Lord of the universe. There is much debate among theologians about what it means to be created in the "image of God." What we do know is that when God speaks of making man in His image and in His likeness, He was speaking of His character, His nature, His power and authority to rule, govern and create! God is Spirit; man is spirit. God is Creator; man was given the ability to create. God is the "I AM" and all He does flows from His being. Man, created in God's image, is called to *be*. Man was not created to *do* a job! He was given dominion and responsibility in the earth because of who he was created to *be*.

From the very beginning of man's existence, he looked like God and he walked with God; he was in relationship with God. God then created the woman and gave her to Adam. The two of them walked in relationship with God and with one another, and it was out of this relationship that man was able to reflect the image of God in the earth. God and Adam were friends! We read that God was accustomed to spending time with Adam; Adam lived in the presence of God. The garden was created, in a sense, to be "their" place! It was a place of fellowship, communion, and relationship with God! It was a place of fruitfulness and plenty! It was a place of tranquility and peace! It was a place of fulfillment! It was the place where they could simply *be* with God! It was from this state of *being* that all else flowed.

Created As Worshipers

Adam was not created to worship God, but *as a worshiper*. All that he was called to *do* —from having dominion to tending the garden to naming the animals — was to flow from that state of *being*. And so it is with us; for you see, man was created to *be,* not to *do*! We were not designed to *do* worship but we were designed to *be* worshipers. We are worshipers by design! It may seem like a minor point, but it is a point that will help us return to the place of worship and to the relationship that God intended.

What, then, is a worshiper? I define a worshiper as **one who is intimately acquainted with, and has a daily relationship with God exhibited through obedience.**

God desires for us to be intimately acquainted with Him and to have a daily relationship with Him that is demonstrated by our obedience to Him. God's intention from the beginning was to *be* in relationship with His most precious creation — Man! Adam lived as a worshiper and all was good! Adam and Eve were in perfect relationship with God to fulfill purpose and destiny. What more could they have wanted? One would think they would have been content! And I believe that they were until something happened that changed the relationship between God and man.

They Wanted Something They Already Had

Genesis 3 tells us of Adam's fatal decision, a decision that changed a relationship that was meant to last forever. Adam's decision was not based on a need; it was based on a desire that was birthed out of deception. His decision to disobey God was based on the thought that he was missing out on something, that God was keeping something from him. Adam was deceived! This thought was planted in his mind and in the mind of the woman by satan. Let's look at this passage more closely to gain a better under-standing of what happened.

> *"Now the serpent was more crafty than any beast of the field which the Lord God had made. And he said to the woman, "Indeed, has God said, 'You shall not eat from any tree of the garden'?" And the woman said to the serpent, "From the fruit of the trees of the garden we may eat; but from the fruit of the tree which is in the middle of the garden, God has said, 'You shall not eat from it or touch it, lest you die.'" And the serpent said to the*

woman, *"You surely shall not die!* ***"For God knows that in the day you eat from it your eyes will be opened, and you will be like God, knowing good and evil.***" *When the woman saw that the tree was good for food, and that it was a delight to the eyes, and that the tree was desirable to make one wise, she took from its fruit and ate; and she gave also to her husband with her, and he ate."* (Genesis 3:1-6 emphasis added)

Through the serpent, satan entered into a conversation with the woman and simply posed a question that sowed a seed of doubt and distrust. Then he planted this thought: "God is holding back on you! You can be more than you are and God knows it. That's why He doesn't want you to eat of the tree of the knowledge of good and evil." What the woman did not realize was that satan was planting a thought, a seed that, once entertained and acted upon, would produce a harvest of sin and death. He planted the seed of iniquity! It was the very same seed that originated in him while he was in heaven. This is what the Scriptures say about satan before his fall:

"How you have fallen from heaven,
O star of the morning, son of the dawn!
You have been cut down to the earth,
You who have weakened the nations!
"But you said in your heart,
'I will ascend to heaven;

*I will raise my throne above the stars of
    God,
And I will sit on the mount of assembly
In the recesses of the north.
'I will ascend above the heights of the
    clouds;*
I will make myself like the Most High.
*But you are brought down to the grave, to
    the depths of the pit.* (Isaiah 14:12-14
    emphasis added)

Ezekiel 28:13-15 says this concerning lucifer:

*Thou hast been in Eden the garden of God;
every precious stone was thy covering, the
sardius, topaz, and the diamond, the beryl,
the onyx, and the jasper, the sapphire, the
emerald, and the carbuncle, and gold: the
workmanship of thy tabrets and of thy pipes
was prepared in thee in the day that thou wast
created. Thou art the anointed cherub that
covereth; and I have set thee so: thou wast
upon the holy mountain of God; thou hast
walked up and down in the midst of the stones
of fire.* **Thou wast perfect in thy ways from
the day that thou wast created, till iniquity
was found in thee.** (KJV emphasis added)

It was that thought — *I will be like God* — that
led to lucifer's rebellion and led to his expulsion from
heaven. It was this same thought that led to the man
and woman's sin of rebellion and to their eventual

expulsion from the Garden. What was the motivation that caused them to rebel? It's really quite simple: *They wanted to be like God!* Without knowing it, they had taken on the same attitude that originated in the heart of lucifer (Isaiah 14:14). This was the most cunning and deceiving trick of the enemy. He tricked them into believing that they were missing out on something that they already had! They already had God's image and His likeness! Their one act of rebellion awakened something inside of them that is now inside every man— the perverted desire not to be just *like* God, but rather to *be* God!

We know that Adam's choice brought with it death or separation from God. Man could no longer derive his sense of being from that connection with God. I believe it would be accurate to say that since man was now separated from God by the sin of rebellion and since now he sought to be "god," his only sense of fulfillment was found in what he *did*, for it's only in God that we have our *being*. I believe that is why human beings have become so focused on what we *do*. It gives us a sense of meaning and value. I also believe that is why worship has become more an act rather than a state of being.

The desire to be "god" is one that is not satisfied except when exalting one's self. We must recognize and acknowledge that this small seed is in every man — even in our own hearts! It is what drives us to seek out attention, fame, fortune and notoriety! It is what causes us to exalt ourselves or allow ourselves to be exalted above others. It is what causes many to go all their lives in search of affirmation. It is the prevailing spirit in the world today! And it is an insatiable appetite that can never be satisfied, but can only be mastered by putting it to death!

The Apostle Paul addresses this by telling us in Romans 12:1-2 not to be conformed to this world. He writes: *"I urge you therefore, brethren, by the mercies of God, to present your bodies a living and holy sacrifice, acceptable to God, which is your spiritual service of worship. And do not be conformed to this world, but be transformed by the renewing of your mind, that you may prove what the will of God is, that which is good and acceptable and perfect."*

The Apostle John, in his first epistle, warns the church about the lust for the world's things when he writes: *"Do not love the world, nor the things in the world. If anyone loves the world, the love of the Father is not in him. For all that is in the world, the lust of the flesh and the lust of the eyes and the boastful pride of life, is not from the Father, but is from the world. And the world is passing away, and also its lusts; but the one who does the will of God abides forever." 1 John 2:15-17*

It is this very subtle attitude and appetite that has crept into the worship life of the church. The term "worship" has now become a music genre. We have begun to define worship as a musical style. It has become a category in the music industry where many are now slotted for their musical style. Not only that, but we now define worshipers by what they *do*, not by who they are.

If we are not aware of this, we may be driven to do things in the name of "worship" that are not really worship at all. Because we have believed worship (and life itself) is about *doing*, we have become results-oriented and results-driven. But God never intended that we would be driven by anything, but rather led by His Spirit! Led by His Presence! This is why I challenge the statement *"We were created to worship God"* because it suggests that we were created to *do* something rather than to *be* someone. And while this statement sounds "spiritual," I do not believe it accurately states the reason for our existence. It is just slightly off, and as a result of accepting it as absolute truth, we have become like a ship that has set sail with its coordinates slightly off. If the coordinates are off by the slightest degree as the ship embarks on its journey, it remains off course and misses the mark! It cannot reach its ultimate destination! All because it was slightly off when it started! It is now time to turn the ship called worship by resetting the coordinates so that we reach our intended destination – the Lord Himself!

God's intention is the same today as it was when He created Adam. His desire is that we are intimately acquainted and have a daily relationship with Him that is seen in our total obedience to Him. It is His desire that out of that relationship, out of that state of *being*, we reflect His glory and mirror His image in the earth and fulfill the Genesis 1 commission. That's why He sent His Son, Jesus. In life, Jesus exemplified what it meant to be a true worshiper. In His death and resurrection, He opened the door that we might enter back into right relationship with the Father! He died and rose again so that we might become worshipers again!

As we continue to explore "the truth about worship," I believe that eventually we will see that it is so much more than we have allowed it to become!

CHAPTER TWO

Who Taught You That?

My mind flashes back to the 1980's and 90's. It was about that time that a new focus on worship came to the forefront of the church in a way we'd not seen before. A new genre of music — worship music — became popular, especially through such ministries as Integrity Music; books on worship began to line the shelves of bookstores more than ever before; all across the nation and around the world worship conferences and workshops were being held and the attendance was always high. Everyone wanted to be a part of the "new thing" that God was doing. Of course, worship is not a new thing – it's the very thing that has been taking place in heaven before time began. I believe that the 1980's was the beginning of the Holy Spirit bringing the church back to the place and heart of true worship.

There were classes and books on how to lead worship, how to develop worship teams, how to "flow in the Spirit," how to write worship choruses. And while there was teaching concerning the heart of the worshiper, much of the teaching focused more on the art rather than the heart. I will be the first to acknowledge that much of what was taught was good! My life and ministry were dramatically changed as a result of sitting under the worship teaching of some incredibly anointed men and women of God — true worshipers, *intimately acquainted with God and having a daily relationship with Him exhibited through their obedience.* But as I reflect on my conversation with the individual who insisted her pastor was not a worshiper, I can't help but ask how we arrived at that place. What has been taught that would cause someone to come to such a conclusion? It has caused me to rethink many of the things I have taught in the area of worship, and it has also caused me to consider some things to which I had never really given much thought.

We were taught almost everything we know! Have you ever taken a moment to ponder that thought? From the moment you were born you have been the recipient of information, whether by observation, example, or formal education. Think about it! Someone told you what your name is. You were taught how to read, write, spell, add, subtract, multiply, divide, and much of the time, you never stopped to ask, "How do I know this is true?" We trust that the information we receive is accurate and true! We frame our thoughts, logic, perceptions, decisions, opinions, conclusions and our actions on the information we have been taught over our lifetime. But what if the information we were taught was not accurate and led us to a wrong conclusion? It could lead to the misdirected application of a principle or practice.

There are so many factors that influence us and how we filter the information we receive. We are influenced by culture, age, ethnicity, experience, preferences and prejudices.

We are influenced by what we have seen. All of these can affect how we process and apply what we are taught. I believe this is what has happened as it relates to worship and the worship life of the church. The result has been that many people can *imitate* what they have seen and heard. They know the worship jargon; they have all the worship forms. They are able to *do* worship. But that is not what God desires of us! All too often the worship life of the church has been reduced to form and even at times to ritual. Is it possible that in all of our teaching and our pursuit of revelation, we have unintentionally arrived in a place not much different than the religious leaders in Jesus' day? Over the years, we have taught worship as an expression, worship as an art form, and yes, worship as a lifestyle. Somewhere in the process, people have concluded that it is in the *doing* more than it is in *being*.

Vain Worship

When *doing,* as it relates to worship, over-rides *being* a worshiper, we produce what the Word describes as "vain worship." It is worship that is meaningless, empty, useless. I find it interesting that the Greek root of the word we translate "vain" actually means "manipulation." Is it possible that "worship" that is more about *doing* than *being* is a form of manipulation and not worship at all?

God, through the prophet Isaiah, addressed a people who had learned the right things to say and do, but who were not sincere in what they were speaking. They were a people whose actions did not flow from their being or from their heart. Isaiah 29:14 says: *"These people come near to me with their mouth and honor me with their lips, but their hearts are far from me.* ***Their worship of me is made up only of rules taught by men."*** (emphasis added)

You hypocrites! Isaiah was right when he prophesied about you:

> "'These people honor me with their lips,
> but their hearts are far from me.
> ***They worship me in vain;***
> ***their teachings are but rules taught by men.'***
> (Matthew 15:7-9 NIV emphasis added)

Jesus was speaking to the religious leaders of His day. He was confronting them about their attitudes and even rebuking them for their mishandling of the people and the Word. Rather than leading the people closer to God, the Pharisees were actually leading the people further away from Him and what He wanted for them by insisting that they follow the "traditions of the elders." Through their teachings the Pharisees set themselves up as the absolute authorities, the spiritual elite, an exclusive group. It was a perversion of the law! They taught a doctrine that was full of rules and regulations to benefit themselves. *The Message: The Bible in Contemporary Language* says it this way:

Frauds! Isaiah's prophecy of you hit the bull's-eye: These people make a big show of saying the right thing, but their heart isn't in it. They act like they're worshiping me, but they don't mean it. They just use me as a cover for teaching whatever suits their fancy."

When Jesus addressed them, He was addressing the fact that they had placed form and ritual over conditions of the heart. He was addressing *the deception of religion*!

The deception of religion is that it has no real affect on the heart. It is purely an external exercise that gives the appearance of a relationship with God that does not really exist! True worship can only come from the heart. There is no real meaningful relationship without the heart being involved!

In the times in which we now live, we too often see this same reality: *"They worship me in vain; their teachings are but rules taught by men."*

The Body of Christ is filled with hundreds of denominations. Many of them are based, in part, on the doctrines and theologies of men! While there are certain truths that can be found in many of these denominations, you can still see how man's input sometimes makes it more about rules and regulations than a relationship with the living God! It is becoming more and more evident that many are attending churches today based on their personal preference, lifestyle and style of worship, rather than being truly led by the Holy Spirit to the place God has chosen for them, where He knows they will grow in their maturity as a believer and in their relationship with Him!

In our attempt to reach *all* people we have allowed ourselves to create a church culture in which one only needs to abide by the rules to be one of the group. We say, "We will tailor our services to fit *you*! We will cater to *your* tastes in music and worship style." We have said in so many words, "Have it *your* way!" The problem with this approach is that it is possible for an individual to now attend a church and never have a real relationship with God!

On the other side, in our attempt to return to what we have believed to be the "heart of worship," we have implied that in order to truly be worshipers, we must sing a certain kind of song, we must have the right mix of "praise" choruses and "worship" choruses, we must say certain words. We have abandoned some of the older traditions of the church and incorporated what we have felt to be the new and innovative things. So we have removed the hymnal and replaced it with Power Point. We have exchanged the organ for a keyboard and guitar. We have moved from devotional service to worship service. We have added worship teams. And we have used these things to define worship and to measure who is a worshiping church and who is not. And yet with all these well-meaning changes, we can still be guilty of "vain worship."

You see, there really is no difference in singing a song out of a hymnbook or singing a song that is projected on a screen. The real difference is in the heart of the person singing. A person who sings "worship" songs can be just as religious as those he *thinks* are religious because they sing out of a hymnal. And the person singing out of the hymnal can be more of a worshiper than the one gazing at the projector screen, but who is not really engaged at a heart level. God knows the difference! The psalmist David knew it was about the heart when he proclaimed:

> *"**I will give thee thanks with my whole heart**: Before the gods will I sing praises unto thee."* (Psalm 138:1 emphasis added)
> *"Praise ye Jehovah. **I will give thanks unto Jehovah with my whole heart**, in the council of the upright, and in the congregation."* (Psalm 111:1 emphasis added)

Singing "worship" songs does not make you a worshiper! Having a worship team does not make you a worshiping church! All of that can become religious exercise if we are not intentional to keep our hearts engaged in the exchange and remain in passionate pursuit of the One we are worshipping — JESUS! It is our daily relationship with Jesus that makes our worship of God genuine and authentic.

I believe the church has entered a season in which the Holy Spirit is confronting us about the things we have taught that in many ways have moved us away from a worship relationship and a worship life to a place more focused on worship activity. If we are going to help bring about change in the Body of Christ, it must start with changing our own models, our vocabulary, and our teachings on worship.

Are We In Or Are We Out?

Over the years, many of us have taught on worship using three Old Testament structures as worship models. These three structures, the tabernacle of Moses (Exodus 35-40), the tabernacle of David (2 Samuel 6:17) and Solomon's temple (2 Chronicles 2-5) with their Outer Court, Holy Place and Most Holy Place or Holy of Holies, are replete with symbolism, revelation and application. Each article, each piece of furniture, and all of the materials used have symbolic and prophetic meaning.

- **Outer Court**: brass, altar of sacrifice, laver, flesh, blood, death, judgment
- **Inner Court**: gold and wood, table of show bread, lamp stand, altar of incense, mixture of spirit and flesh, fellowship, illumination
- **Holy of Holies:** All Gold, the Ark of the Covenant, All HIM, Deity, Reverence, Glory (Kabod-weighty, heaviness), Stillness, Rest

In many of my teachings on worship, I have taught that these structures and their contents represent what I would call our progression in worship. We start from the Outer Court, work our way into the Inner Court and ultimately make our way to the Holy of Holies or Secret Place. I have begun to wonder about the validity of some of this teaching and whether it has even hindered our worship life in light of further understanding of the redemptive work of Christ that gives us continual access into the Presence of God.

Some years ago I read the book *Secrets of The Most Holy Place* by Don Nori, the owner of Destiny Image Publishing. The book changed my life and inspired me to write a song entitled "Within the Veil." The lyrics speak to us about learning to live in that secret place, knowing we have a dwelling place in Him not based on anything that you or I have done, but because of the finished work of Jesus Christ. The words read:

> The works of my own hands no longer
>   matter;
> The arm of flesh, though strong, is all too
>   frail.
> What used to be my strength is now my
>   weakness
> As I stand before the Lord within the veil.
> The war that raged within is finally over;
> The struggle to find peace is realized.
> The One who shed His blood for me is
>   calling,
> Calling me to come where He is and abide.
> Within the veil I see Jesus;
> His light consumes my soul.
> The veil of my own heart has been torn
>   away;

My life will never be the same;
I've found the place where He abides;
It's life within the veil.
My eyes behold the only King of Glory;
I hear His voice so gentle, yet so strong:
"The blood of My own Son has made you
    holy;
Now come and sit with me where you
    belong."
Within the veil I see Jesus;
His light consumes my soul.
The veil of my own heart has been torn
    away;
My life will never be the same;
I've found the place where He abides;
It's life within the veil.

The psalmist wrote about this "life within the veil" in Psalm 91:1, 2:

*He that **dwelleth (lives)** in the secret place of the Most High shall abide under the shadow of the Almighty. I will say of Jehovah, He is my refuge and my fortress; My God, in whom I trust.* (ASV emphasis added)

I have come to realize that God is not looking for visitors; He wants residents. When Jesus died on the cross, the veil was removed giving us full access.

Having therefore such a hope, we use great boldness of speech, and are not as Moses, *who put a veil upon his face, that the children of Israel should not look stedfastly on the end of that which was passing away: but their minds were hardened: for until this very day at the reading of the old covenant the same veil remaineth, it not being revealed to them that it is done away in Christ. But unto this day, whensoever Moses is read, a veil lieth upon their heart. **But whensoever it shall turn to the Lord, the veil is taken away.** Now the Lord is the Spirit: and where the Spirit of the Lord is, **there is liberty**. But we all, with unveiled face beholding as in a mirror the glory of the Lord, are transformed into the same image from glory to glory, even as from the Lord the Spirit.* (2 Corinthians 3:12-17 emphasis added)

Jesus not only gave us access to the Holy of Holies, but through His shed blood we can live (reside, abide, stay) in the Presence of the Almighty! It is in His presence that we are transformed from glory to glory! The veil of our heart was removed the day we accepted Jesus as our Savior and Lord!

When we teach about worship using the models of the tabernacles of Moses and of David and Solomon's temple, we present a teaching that can convey that we have to work our way into the presence of God. This often leads us to move through corporate worship with that thought in mind. We feel we have to sing a certain number of songs or find the right balance between fast and slow songs before we can access the presence of God! With each song we are working our way closer into His presence. Can you see how it just doesn't seem quite right? Not if we believe that Jesus made a way for us to *live* in the presence of Almighty God!

Worship is not a destination! It is a lifestyle that flows from dwelling in the very Presence of the Lord. The worship life of the believer is living with the awareness that we are daily in that Presence. It is living in the reality that we are in Him and He is in us. When we worship Him, we are not trying to work our way into His presence. We are acknowledging that we are already in His Presence and our worship of Him is what gives us access to relate to Him. He is our dwelling place! We are His dwelling place! He is our habitation! We are His habitation!

CHAPTER THREE

What Does It Take?

*W*hat *does it take to worship God?* As we make this shift, as we reset our worship "coordinates," it becomes necessary to ask this question. And we must examine carefully our response. While many may answer by saying that it takes a heart given over to God, far too many still place an emphasis on the form. "We need gifted musicians and singers. We need dancers, flags and banners! And of course, we need a great sound system!" All of these things are wonderful gifts and tools that help us express our worship to our heavenly Father, Who truly is worthy of it. But those tools, in and of themselves, are not the essence of true worship; they only have significance when used by a worshiper.

What does it take to be a worshiper of God? Considering our definition of a worshiper, we realize that to focus on the elements of music and the arts is to reduce worship to something less than God intended and something far less than He deserves. If a worshiper is one who is intimately acquainted with and has a daily relationship with God exhibited through a life of obedience, we must move beyond songs, instruments, banners and art to something deeper and grander; we must move to something that encompasses all of life.

First Mentioned

What does it take to be a worshiper of God? Again we must return to the Word of God. While we have established the fact that Adam was created as a worshiper, the Bible does not give us much detail on Adam's "worship" life that aids us in answering the question set before us. I believe that God has never been without a worshiper in the earth. Certainly, if we examine the lives of such individuals as Abel, Enoch, Noah we may conclude that each of these men were intimately acquainted with and had a daily relationship with God, exhibited through obedience. They were worshipers! But in order for us to gain greater insight into what it takes to be a worshiper of God, we must use the Law of First Mention, a principle that states the first time a word or idea is mentioned in scripture is significant, for it sets a foundation and framework for any other time the word is used throughout the scriptures.

We first see the word "worship" used in connection with Abraham.

The Call to Worship

Abraham was a worshiper! We read in Genesis 12 of God's invitation to Abram, an idol worshiper, to enter into covenant relationship with Him.

Now the Lord said to Abram, "Go forth from your country, And from your relatives And from your father's house, To the land which I will show you; And I will make you a great nation, And I will bless you, And make your name great; And so you shall be a blessing; And I will bless those who bless you, And the one who curses you I will curse. And in you all the families of the earth shall be blessed" (Genesis 12: 1-3).

It is here that God begins to share His heart with Abraham and His desire to bless him. God was looking for relationship! He was looking for a worshiper! I believe that every event in Abraham's life was designed to develop within him the heart of a worshiper.

In Genesis 22, we find the account of Abraham offering up his son Isaac. This is where we first see the word "worship" used. *"And Abraham said to his young men stay here with the donkey, I and the lad will go yonder; and we will **worship** and return to you"* (verse 5 emphasis added). It is important to note that there is no mention of music; there was nothing musical or artistic about this act. The Bible doesn't say that Abraham had a musical instrument. There is no mention of them singing a song on their way up the mountain. And yet before Abraham headed up the mountain, he said to his servants, "We are going to *worship* and then return!" I believe when we look at this passage of scripture, we can detect three factors that are foundational truths as it relates to the worship life of the believer. These truths are important for us to reemphasize.

Without Faith It is Impossible to Worship God

The first thing we observe as Abraham responded to God in worship is *faith*. Abraham is known as the "father of faith," but he did not start out as a man of faith. The journey that led up to the offering up his son was a faith-building journey. From chapter 12 to chapter 22 of Genesis, we see the journey of faith that Abraham walked. And, yes, we know he stumbled along the way. But by the time he is asked to make the ultimate sacrifice, Abraham has become a man of great faith! It was a faith forged over years and years of walking with God and seeing the faithfulness of God. Abraham had grown in his relationship, in his faith and in his ability to trust God!

Abraham was speaking words of faith when he told his servants *"The lad and I will go yonder and we will worship and return to you."*

Worship takes faith! Keep in mind, Abraham knew exactly what God was requiring of him. He acted in complete faith. We must have faith in order to worship God. The Scriptures tell us in Hebrews

11:6, *"Without faith it is impossible to please God."*
The Scriptures also tell us *"he that comes to God must first believe that he is and that he is a rewarder of those who diligently seek him."* Every man is given the measure of faith. Why? Because without faith, it is impossible to worship God! Walking in and living a life of faith is an act of worship. In the book of Romans, we read that Abraham glorified (worshiped) God *through his faith.* Romans 4:19 - 20 says, *"And without being weakened in faith he considered his own body now as good as dead and the deadness of Sarah's womb; yet looking unto the promise of God, he wavered not through unbelief, but grew strong through faith, giving glory to God, being fully persuaded that what He had promised, he was able also to perform."*

I don't believe that Abraham walked around saying, "Praise the Lord! To God be the glory!" as he waited for the manifestation of the promise. It was his consistent walk of faith that glorified God! That was an act of worship! God gets glory when we exercise our faith, as we walk it out, trusting Him in every situation even when it seems impossible! The worship life of the believer is a life of faith in God! Faith that He has everything under His control, no matter what things look like! Faith that He will do exactly what He has promised! Faith that our steps are ordered! Faith that in all things, He is worthy of our worship! Abraham grew to trust God this way. We have the same opportunity.

Obedience is Better than Sacrifice

The second thing we see as Abraham responded to God in worship is *obedience*. Abraham not only grew in faith, but he also grew to be a man of obedience. When God first called Abraham, he was not totally obedient to the leading of God. Abraham did not know this God who called him from Ur of the Chaldees, and for a long while he lived his life by taking measures into his own hands. When he thought his life was in danger, he asked Sarah to lie and say she was his sister; God intervened so that Abraham would not make a mistake and bring judgment on the king at that time. Later Abraham took matters into his own hands again when, with Sarah's encouragement, he slept with Hagar to produce the son he believed would be the son of promise. After Ishmael was born, God came to Abraham and told him that Ishmael would not be his heir. When Sarah later insisted that Abraham send Hagar and Ishmael away, it was really in obedience to the Lord that he did so. Abraham had learned obedience and that obedience would be tested.

True worship involves obedience: obedience to God, obedience to His word, obedience to His voice, obedience to His will, and obedience to His way. In First Samuel 15, God dealt with King Saul's disobedience. Saul, a man who had a poor self image, was more concerned about what people thought about him than walking in obedience to God's Word. God had instructed Saul, through the prophet Samuel, to destroy the Amalekites and spare nothing. Saul fought against the Amalekites, but he did not destroy them as God had commanded. When Samuel realized that Saul had not been obedient to God, he approached Saul, asking why he had not obeyed the word of the Lord. Saul's fear of the people caused him to disobey God and to offer up burnt offerings and sacrifices.

Samuel's response to Saul speaks to the importance of obedience in our worship. He said, *"Has the Lord as much delight in burnt offerings and sacrifices, as in obeying the voice of the Lord? Behold to obey is better than sacrifice and to heed than the fat of rams."* Saul's disobedience cost him the kingdom. He thought he could offer up what *he* wanted, and it would be acceptable. But without obedience, the sacrifice meant nothing. He failed to realize that we do not determine what is acceptable to God; God does. To offer anything other than what He has deemed acceptable is an act of disobedience. As worshipers, we must always be mindful of this truth. Our offering, our sacrifice, our song, our dance if not given in obedience to the Lord may satisfy something in us, but it is not worship; it is not received by the Lord.

There is no true worship without obedience. A life of obedience before the Lord is a life of worship. It was Adam's disobedience in the Garden of Eden that separated him, and ultimately you and me, from God. It was Jesus obedience to the Father, even unto death, that gave us opportunity to enter back into a right relationship with God (Romans 5:19). Our obedience starts by acknowledging our sins, repenting of our sins, accepting God's Son, Jesus, as our Savior and Lord, receiving His Holy Spirit, and living an obedient life according to His word. That's the worship life!

A Living Sacrifice

The third thing we see as Abraham responded to God in worship is *sacrifice*! Ever since the fall of man God has required a sacrifice. When God entered into covenant with Abraham, that covenant was sealed by a sacrifice (Genesis 15:7-18). And now God was asking His friend, Abraham, to offer his son as a "sacrifice!" There is no true worship without sacrifice. I heard a very wealthy person once say when we give an offering to the Lord, He is not looking at what we give, but rather how much we have left! The level and depth of our worship is determined by the level and depth of our sacrifice. King David understood this. He said, *"I will not offer to the Lord something that has cost me nothing!"* (2 Samuel 24:24) He knew the importance of a sacrifice and the blessing that came from giving it.

Romans 12:1, 2 tells us that we are to present our bodies as living *sacrifices* wholly and acceptable unto God which is our reasonable *worship*. We now present ourselves as a living sacrifice to the Lord instead of bulls and lambs. But it is not man's nature to sacrifice; man, for the most part, is selfish and can be self-centered. To truly worship God takes dying to self. It takes a willingness to sacrifice our own desires for His, a willingness to sacrifice our will for His, and a willingness to sacrifice our way for His. I believe

that the words of this song say it best. As worshipers
of God, this should be the cry of our heart:

> Lord, I want to be like You;
> That is my heart's desire.
> I want to know You face to face,
> Not from afar.
> To die to my own will and lay ambition
>   down;
> To wholly seek Your face
> While walking in Your grace.
> Take my life, let it be
> Wholly unto Thee.
> Take my life, let it be
> Wholly unto Thee
> A living sacrifice; a living sacrifice
> A living sacrifice, Lord.
> Lord, I give You my life.
> Lord, I give You my life.

Psalms 50: 5 says, "*Gather to me the Godly ones,
those that have made a covenant with me by sacrifice.*" To sacrifice means to surrender or lay down
our own agendas, our own plans. It is through our
personal sacrifice that we demonstrate to God that
we are willing to die to self and place Him first in our
lives. We must understand that worship is not about
us and our preference. It is about God and Him alone!
And we must reiterate that God is the One who deter-
mines the sacrifice.

Abraham was created *as* a worshiper, but he
became a true worshiper of God as walked the path

God had ordained for him and as he learned to trust the Lord in all things. He grew to become a worshiper over the course of many, many years. It wasn't his gifts, his talents, his song or his dance that made Abraham a worshiper; it was his faith, his obedience and his willingness to sacrifice even that which God had blessed him with. He was a worshiper because of his willingness to grow to know God in the most intimate ways and to become a "friend of God."

CHAPTER FOUR

Free To Be a Worshiper

From Adam to Noah to Abraham down through time to you and to me, God's desire has been to bring man into the same intimate love relationship He has with His Son, Jesus. He created us as worshipers and He calls us, as He called Abraham, into covenant relationship. As we live our lives as those who are *intimately acquainted with and have a daily relationship with God exhibited through obedience,* we see God faithfully respond.

When God called Abraham into covenant with Him, His promise was not only to Abraham; the Father was looking beyond Abraham. You see, it was never about an individual. God's desire is to have a family of worshipers, a nation of worshipers who would walk in covenant relationship with Him and then would fill the earth with worshipers who reflected His glory and fulfilled the purpose and destiny spoken of in the first chapter of Genesis. His goal was to restore what Adam had forfeited through Abraham and his seed.

God Remembers His Promise

In covenant love, God demonstrated His faithfulness to His friend, Abraham. Some 600 years after Abraham was called from Ur, his descendents were enslaved by the Egyptians, just as the Lord had told him. We read these words:

> *Now it came about in the course of those many days that the king of Egypt died. And the sons of Israel sighed because of the bondage, and they cried out; and their cry for help because of their bondage rose up to God. So God heard their groaning;* ***and God remembered His covenant with Abraham, Isaac, and Jacob.*** *And God saw the sons of Israel, and God took notice of them.* (Exodus 2:23-25 emphasis added)

God remembered His promise to Abraham, and He set out to fulfill that promise when He called Moses. While Moses was not sure of the call, God was sure that Moses was the man for the task! Moses' first encounter with God was a worship experience.

> *"And the angel of the Lord appeared to him in a blazing fire from the midst of a bush; and he looked, and behold, the bush was burning with fire, yet the bush was not consumed.*

So Moses said, "I must turn aside now, and see this marvelous sight, why the bush is not burned up." When the Lord saw that he turned aside to look, God called to him from the midst of the bush, and said, "Moses, Moses!" And he said, "Here I am." Then He said, "Do not come near here; remove your sandals from your feet, for the place on which you are standing is holy ground." He said also, "I am the God of your father, the God of Abraham, the God of Isaac, and the God of Jacob." Then Moses hid his face, for he was afraid to look at God. And the Lord said, "I have surely seen the affliction of My people who are in Egypt, and have given heed to their cry because of their taskmasters, for I am aware of their sufferings. So I have come down to deliver them from the power of the Egyptians, and to bring them up from that land to a good and spacious land, to a land flowing with milk and honey, to the place of the Canaanite and the Hittite and the Amorite and the Perizzite and the Hivite and the Jebusite." (Exodus 3:2-8)

It was out of this worship experience that God shared the mission with Moses as well as His reason for setting His people free. God wanted them free so they could worship Him!

Therefore, come now, and I will send you to Pharaoh, so that you may bring My people, the sons of Israel, out of Egypt." But Moses said to God, "Who am I, that I should go to Pharaoh, and that I should bring the sons of Israel out of Egypt?" And He said, "Certainly I will be with you, and this shall be the sign to you that it is I who have sent you: when you have brought the people out of Egypt, you shall worship God at this mountain." (Exodus 3:10-12)

"Let My People Go"

It is over the next twelve chapters of Exodus that we see God use Moses as His voice to Pharaoh. The message was always the same, *"Let My people go, so that they may worship Me!"* At least six times Moses spoke this same directive to Pharaoh! It was God's intent to bring them out of bondage and to bring them into a place of relationship (worship) with Him. He wanted to relate to His people and have them relate to Him. He was returning them to their created purpose. Man had been created in freedom as a worshiper. The trappings of Egypt, symbolic of the world, had made it virtually impossible for him to fulfill that purpose. The goal of freedom, of deliverance, of salvation is that we may live as worshipers of God.

We know the story. After encountering the true and living God through the ten plagues, Pharaoh set the children of Israel free. The Lord led them to Mount Sinai where He invited them into covenant relationship with Him. It was there that He invited them to be His betrothed, to be His bride. He invited them to be His treasure, His nation of kings and priests who would show forth His glory to the entire world. He invited them to become true worshipers.

In Exodus 19, God instructed Moses to have the people prepare themselves because He was coming to speak to them.

> *"The Lord also said to Moses, "Go to the people and consecrate them today and tomorrow, and let them wash their garments; and let them be ready for the third day, for on the third day the Lord will come down on Mount Sinai in the sight of all the people. And you shall set bounds for the people all around, saying, 'Beware that you do not go up on the mountain or touch the border of it; whoever touches the mountain shall surely be put to death. 'No hand shall touch him, but he shall surely be stoned or shot through; whether beast or man, he shall not live.' When the ram's horn sounds a long blast, they shall come up to the mountain." So Moses went down from the mountain to the people and consecrated the people, and they washed their garments."* (Exodus 19:10-15)

Unfortunately, the people failed to see this as a personal invitation to worship. Fear blinded them, making them unable to see the magnitude of God's love for them and His heart's desire for them to *be* with Him. They failed to answer the call to *be* a nation of worshipers, a nation of people intimately acquainted with Him. Instead, in fear, they fled from His presence. They had no desire to know God intimately, and they rejected His invitation! Rather than entering into a personal relationship with Him, they set up a system through which they would relate to God via a mediator. God would now relate to His people through Moses.

God's heart for intimacy with His people has not changed! It is His desire to be close to us and He desires that we would want to be close to Him. He is not looking for us to put on a show for Him by the use of our gifts, talents or abilities. He simply wants us to want to be with Him. God sent Moses as a deliverer to lead His people out of bondage. And He has done the same for us through Jesus Christ.

Jesus, our Deliverer, has set us free from the cruel bondage of an evil taskmaster. He has saved us from the penalty of death that was associated with sin, and has redeemed us from the curse of the law. He set us free to become worshipers! He has set us in heavenly places *in* Christ Jesus! He has done all of this with one purpose in mind: that you and I would spend the rest of our lives in the relationship with Him for which we were created. It is a life in His presence as worshipers! The promise He made to Abraham included you and me. We fulfill that promise when we live as worshipers.

The Introduction of Music and Arts

The first mention of a musical expression by worshipers can found right after the children of Israel crossed the Red Sea. We see in Exodus 15:1-15 that Moses and the people lifted up a spontaneous song while Miriam and the other women offered a spontaneous dance of praise and gratitude to the Lord. This was their first response to having been set free after 430 years of slavery! What a celebration they must have had! Can you imagine being a part of what we could call the first "praise and worship" service?

> *Then Moses and the sons of Israel sang this song to the Lord, and said,*
> *"I will sing to the Lord, for He is highly exalted;*
> *The horse and its rider He has hurled into the sea.*
> *"The Lord is my strength and song,*
> *And He has become my salvation;*
> *This is my God, and I will praise Him;*
> *My father's God, and I will extol Him.*
> *"The Lord is a warrior;*
> *The Lord is His name.* (Exodus 15:1-3)

And Miriam the prophetess, Aaron's sister, took the timbrel in her hand, and all the women went out after her with timbrels and with dancing. And Miriam answered them,
> *"Sing to the Lord, for He is highly exalted;*
> *The horse and his rider He has hurled into the sea."* (Exodus 15:20-21)

Bible scholars believe it is most likely that Moses was trained as a musician while in Pharaoh's house.

We know that he is the author of a number of psalms. And, yet while we see this musical expression here at the Red Sea, we don't read that singers and musicians were a part of the worship in the Tabernacle. According the Bible scholars, more than 400 years would pass before we see music instituted as a prominent part of the worship experience.

David Was a Worshiper

One of the most influential worship models for the church today is the "Davidic" model. The term speaks to worship that is musical, celebratory, and worship that includes dance, banners, flags. It is worship that is full of excitement and passion, reflective of David, who was a passionate worshiper.

One of the first accounts that mention David's relationship with God is found in 1 Samuel 16.

> *Saul's servants then said to him, "Behold now, an evil spirit from God is terrorizing you. Let our lord now command your servants who are before you. Let them seek a man who is a skillful player on the harp; and it shall come about when the evil spirit from God is on you, that he shall play the harp with his hand, and you will be well." So Saul said to his servants, "Provide for me now a man who can play well, and bring him to me." Then one of the young men answered and said, "Behold, I have seen a son of Jesse the Bethlehemite who is a skillful musician, a mighty man of*

*valor, a warrior, one prudent in speech, and
a handsome man; **and the Lord is with him.***"
(verses 15-18 emphasis added)

Notice the last thing the servant said about David
— *"and the Lord is with him."* Of all the things he
said about David, that was the most important thing!
It is that statement that tells us that David was a
worshiper! He was intimately acquainted with God
and had a daily relationship with Him, exhibited
through his obedience!

David was a worshiper who happened to be a
musician. He was not a worshiper because he was
a musician; he was a worshiper because he knew
God and God knew him! *David assigned musicians to worship before the Lord because he was a
musician.*

David worshiped God out of the unique gifts and
talents given to him. When David wanted to establish
a place of worship for God, he established it based
on his personal worship expression! David was a
musician. So who did he recruit to help him in the
worship expression? He recruited musicians! Let's
look at some of those appointments:

- **1 Chronicles 6:31 (NIV):** *"[The Temple
  Musicians] These are the men David put in
  charge of the music in the house of the LORD
  after the ark came to rest there."*
- **1 Chronicles 9:33 (NIV):** *"Those who were
  musicians, heads of Levite families, stayed
  in the rooms of the temple and were exempt*

from other duties because they were respon-sible for the work day and night."

- **1 Chronicles 15:19 (NIV):** *"The **musicians** Heman, Asaph and Ethan were to sound the bronze cymbals;"*
- **2 Chronicles 5:12 (NIV):** *"All the Levites who were **musicians**—Asaph, Heman, Jeduthun and their sons and relatives—stood on the east side of the altar, dressed in fine linen and playing cymbals, harps and lyres. They were accompanied by 120 priests sounding trumpets."*
- **2 Chronicles 9:11 (NIV):** *"The king used the algumwood to make steps for the temple of the LORD and for the royal palace, and to make harps and lyres for the **musicians**. Nothing like them had ever been seen in Judah."*
- **2 Chronicles 35:15 (NIV):** *"The **musicians**, the descendants of Asaph, were in the places prescribed by David, Asaph, Heman and Jeduthun the king's seer. The gatekeepers at each gate did not need to leave their posts, because their fellow Levites made the prepa-rations for them."*

Worship Is Personal and Worship Is Corporate

God created us to be expressive! He gave each of us gifts and talents that are similar, yet unique! It is the blending of our varied worship expres-sions that create a glimpse of heavenly worship! It is important for us to be open to one another and the diverse worship styles we may have. Some of the most powerful worship experiences recorded have happened in the midst of corporate worship where all of the participants are praising God at once! It is a glorious sight to see and a glorious sound to hear!

There is the personal expression and there is the corporate expression. God desires both!

Our worship of God is both personal and corporate. It is personal because we serve a personal God! He knew you and me before we were born. He knows everything about us! Your personal worship is precious to Him because no one else can offer up the worship that comes from you! Your worship expression is unique to you! All of your life experiences are peculiar to you and each experience plays a part in the way you express your worship to God! And that worship goes beyond our private times spent with the Lord. Our personal worship is lived out in our daily lives! Remember the three factors of worship: faith, obedience and sacrifice? It is our personal walk with the Lord exhibiting these three elements that shows that we are worshipers. It is our personal commitment to live the life of a worshiper that impacts our role and participation in corporate worship.

Our worship is also corporate. As much as we are created to be unique individuals, we are also connected through Jesus Christ. We are the Body of Christ! Ephesians 4:20 says that we are "fitly jointed together." God designed His body to be interdependent. There is a corporate response to God that results in a response from God: the manifestation of His awesome glory! There is a powerful manifestation of

God that happens when we, as His Body, respond to His presence in worship. One of the examples of this is found in 2 Chronicles 5: 11-14:

> *"And when the priests came forth from the holy place (for all the priests who were present had sanctified themselves, without regard to divisions), and all the Levitical singers, Asaph, Heman, Jeduthun, and their sons and kinsmen, clothed in fine linen, with cymbals, harps, and lyres, standing east of the altar, and with them one hundred and twenty priests blowing trumpets in unison when the trumpeters and the singers were to make themselves heard with one voice to praise and to glorify the Lord, and when they lifted up their voice accompanied by trumpets and cymbals and instruments of music, and when they praised the Lord saying, "He indeed is good for His lovingkindness is everlasting," then the house, the house of the Lord, was filled with a cloud, so that the priests could not stand to minister because of the cloud, for the glory of the Lord filled the house of God."*

Our corporate worship, while it may include singing, dancing, and other art forms, is really the result of individuals coming together and adding their unique expression. That expression is an outflow of who we are designed to be – true worshipers!

CHAPTER FIVE

The Act of Worship

We were *designed* to be intimately acquainted with and have a daily relationship with God, exhibited through obedience. We are *"worshipers by design."* God designed all of man's life to be lived in total awareness of His presence. His plan for us was that we live *in* and *from* that Presence. All that we would do – *every act* – would be a direct result of our *being* in His Presence; every act would flow out of our intimate relationship with Him. It was an intentional *act* of disobedience that separated us from God. It took an intentional *act* of obedience to return us to a place of right-standing with God.

As I stated in the last chapter, our worship is both personal and corporate. The corporate expression and display of worship emanates from our personal worship life. It flows out of our daily life of faith, obedience and sacrifice. How we relate to God personally can be seen in how we relate to Him in the corporate setting.

Any relationship between two or more individuals is predicated on spoken or unspoken, written or unwritten rules of engagement. Families have them. Friends have them. Companies have them. Organizations have them. You have them, and I have them. God also has "rules of engagement" that He has set forth in His Word.

Psalm 24:1-6 says:

The earth is the Lord's, and all it contains,
The world, and those who dwell in it.
For He has founded it upon the seas,
And established it upon the rivers.
Who may ascend into the hill of the Lord?
And who may stand in His holy place?
He who has clean hands and a pure heart,
Who has not lifted up his soul to falsehood,
And has not sworn deceitfully.
He shall receive a blessing from the Lord
And righteousness from the God of his
*   salvation.*
This is the generation of those who seek
*   Him,*
Who seek Thy face — even Jacob.

Psalm 100 reads:

Shout joyfully to the Lord, all the earth.
Serve the Lord with gladness;
Come before Him with joyful singing.
Know that the Lord Himself is God;

It is He who has made us, and not we
ourselves;
We are His people and the sheep of His
pasture.
Enter His gates with thanksgiving,
And His courts with praise. Give thanks to
Him; bless His name.
For the Lord is good;
His lovingkindness is everlasting,
And His faithfulness to all generations.

We can see that there are conditions that must be met for one to ascend into the holy hill of the Lord and to enter into His presence!

Here is a more sobering example found in Ezekiel 44:9-16. This is what God had required of the Levites and this was His response to their disobedience:

'Thus says the Lord God, "No foreigner,
uncircumcised in heart and uncircumcised
in flesh, of all the foreigners who are among
the sons of Israel, shall enter My sanctuary.
"But the Levites who went far from Me, when
Israel went astray, who went astray from Me
after their idols, shall bear the punishment for
their iniquity. "Yet they shall be ministers in
My sanctuary, having oversight at the gates
of the house and ministering in the house;
they shall slaughter the burnt offering and the
sacrifice for the people, and they shall stand
before them to minister to them. **"Because**
they ministered to them before their idols

and became a stumbling block of iniquity to the house of Israel, therefore I have sworn against them," declares the Lord God, "that they shall bear the punishment for their iniquity. "And they shall not come near to Me to serve as a priest to Me, nor come near to any of My holy things, to the things that are most holy; but they shall bear their shame and their abominations which they have committed. "Yet I will appoint them to keep charge of the house, of all its service, and of all that shall be done in it.

"But the Levitical priests, the sons of Zadok, who kept charge of My sanctuary when the sons of Israel went astray from Me, shall come near to Me to minister to Me; and they shall stand before Me to offer Me the fat and the blood," declares the Lord God. "They shall enter My sanctuary; they shall come near to My table to minister to Me and keep My charge. (emphasis added)

Even though the veil that once separated man from God has been removed giving us direct access into His Holy Place, we still cannot approach this Holy God any way we please. Throughout the Scriptures we find many passages that help us understand that God has a prescribed way that He wants us to come before Him. It is our response to Him that I call *The Act of Worship!*

The Act of Worship is the doorway that leads us to the proper posture before a Holy God that then gives opportunity for relationship with Him.

Why the *act of worship*? Because it is an *intentional act* and response to a directive given by God. It is an *act of obedience* that nullifies all willful disobedience and that goes beyond our original intent or action. It is through the *act of worship* that we intentionally posture ourselves before God in total submission to Him according to His will and His desire. It is through the *act of worship* that we put to death any sense of pride or arrogance that says we have the right to relate to God on our own terms. It is through the *act of worship* that we demonstrate our total obedience and surrender to a Holy God!

I want to look at three passages of Scripture that will help bring clarity to this thought.

The Proper Posture

The first passage of Scripture can be found in Exodus 3:1-5:

Now Moses was pasturing the flock of Jethro his father-in-law, the priest of Midian; and he led the flock to the west side of the wilderness, and came to Horeb, the mountain of God. And the angel of the Lord appeared to him in a blazing fire from the midst of a bush; and he looked, and behold, the bush was burning with fire, yet the bush was not consumed. So Moses said, "I must turn aside now, and see this marvelous sight, why the bush is not burned up." When the Lord saw that he turned aside to look, God called to him from the midst of the bush, and said, "Moses, Moses!" And he said, "Here I am." **Then He said, "Do not come near here; remove your sandals from your feet, for the place on which you are standing is holy ground."**

It was God Who called Moses. God saved Moses from death when he was a child, and placed him in the care of Pharaoh's daughter. God allowed Moses to grow up in Pharaoh's house and to be raised as a leader. Through an act of anger, Moses killed a man and found himself a fugitive in the desert for 40 years! God used this time to prepare Moses for his destiny. In Exodus 3 we read of Moses' encounter with God on Mount Horeb. It was there that Moses, for the first time, came into the presence of the living God. Notice God's first words to Moses: **"Do not come near here; remove your sandals from your feet, for the place on which you are standing is holy ground."**

It is here that I believe God, in His mercy and grace, helped Moses to understand a truth: *"You can only be in My Presence and relate to Me on My terms!"* Moses did not know God and it was necessary for God to give him the rules of engagement before Moses attempted to interact with Him. He stopped Moses and said. "Don't come any closer! I know I called you here, but you don't really know

Me. Before We can relate to one another, I need you to take off your shoes in acknowledgement that the ground you are standing on is holy!" At that moment, Moses had a choice to make. He could choose to take off his shoes or he could choose not to; he could choose to obey or he could choose not to. His choice was to remove his shoes. I have often wondered what might have happened had Moses chosen differently. Quite honestly, I believe the conversation would have been over and God would have killed him! You see, Moses' response to God's directive was an "*act of worship*." He assumed the *proper posture* (required position) before a Holy God that *then* gave opportunity for relationship (interaction) with Him (God). The "*proper posture*" is the posture or action that God is calling for in that very moment!

Right Attitude, Wrong Posture

The second passage of Scripture I want to look at is found in Joshua 5:13-15. Forty years had passed and Joshua, considered Moses' right-hand man because he remained so close to Moses, had now been chosen as Moses' successor. Moses had failed to obey God at a crucial time in his leadership, and God judged him by not letting him go into the Promised Land. When God had made it clear to Moses that he would not go into the Promised Land, He instructed Moses to lay his hands on Joshua and declare him as the next leader. In Joshua 1, God spoke to Joshua to assure him that just as He had been with Moses, He would now be with Joshua! In essence, He was saying to him, "The same type of relationship I had with Moses, I will now have with you!" Joshua took God at His word and stepped into his role as the new leader. As Joshua moved into a more intimate relationship with God, we see in Joshua 5 the same directive given to him that was given to Moses in his first intimate encounter with God:

Now it came about when Joshua was by Jericho, that he lifted up his eyes and looked, and behold, a man was standing opposite him with his sword drawn in his hand, and Joshua went to him and said to him, "Are you for us or for our adversaries?" And he said, "No, rather I indeed come now as captain of the host of the Lord." And Joshua fell on his face to the earth, and bowed down, and said to him, "What has my lord to say to his servant?" And the captain of the Lord's host said to Joshua, ***"Remove your sandals from your feet, for the place where you are standing is holy."*** *And Joshua did so.* (emphasis added)

Joshua fell on his knees with his face to the ground. He then asked a simple question: *"What has my lord to say to his servant?"* The Lord's response was, *"Remove your sandals from your feet, for the place where you are standing is holy."* Before God would say anything to Joshua, He needed Joshua to assume the *proper posture*! "Take off your shoes; the ground you are on is holy ground!" It was not enough that Joshua had already kneeled down. While it was *a posture*, it was not *the posture* God was requiring at that moment! We know that Joshua responded in obedience and removed his shoes. Had he chosen not to remove his shoes, I believe, as I said with Moses, his leadership role would have been short-lived and perhaps Caleb would have been the next to lead! This *act of worship* positioned Joshua. The *act of worship* is a deliberate attempt to worship and to honor God in the way that pleases Him. It is an adjustment in the moment by the leading of the Holy Spirit! Even if it means changing our current posture, be it a posture of the heart (attitude), a posture of the mind (the way we think it should be), or our physical posture (to stand, sit, kneel, run, dance, shout, be silent).

A few years ago I wrote a song, "Show Me Where You Are Today," that speaks to our need to adjust our posture. Too often we become accustom to doing things a certain way because it worked in the past. We think, "This is how I reached God before. Surely it will work this time. If I kneel or if I sing this chorus, God will respond as He has in the past." And we do what we've always done only to find that God is not in the old and familiar, and He is calling us to step out of our comfort zone to find Him. I have discovered that there are many "secret places" and God at times is calling us to a new place, a new posture, a new song, a new and different response. We must be willing to ask Him to show us where He is in that moment.

I am drawn by the familiar,
Though it does not satisfy

79

The longing in my heart for more of You.
Lord, I hunger for Your Presence;
I am searching for that door
I know in You are places
I have never been before.
Show me, Lord, where You are today;
Your secret place,
Lord, I won't delay
To come where You are;
Show me where You are today.
I have looked in all the places
Where I found You once before;
There are memories of Your fragrance,
But You're not there anymore.
I hear melodies that whisper,
Saying there's an open door.
I know that I am closer
Than I've ever been before.
Show me, Lord, where You are today;
Your secret place,
Lord, I won't delay
To come where You are;
Show me where You are today.

It's Not Just What You Say

Lastly, let's look at John 11:18-35. It is the story Lazarus being raised from the dead, and it is one of the most powerful stories in the New Testament. My focus is not on Lazarus, but rather his sisters, Martha and Mary. Martha and Mary both knew Jesus. We see that Jesus was a frequent guest in their home. On one occasion, He was visiting and Martha became upset because Jesus did not make Mary assist her.

> *Now as they were traveling along, He entered a certain village; and a woman named Martha welcomed Him into her home.* **And she had a sister called Mary, who moreover was listening to the Lord's word, seated at His feet. But Martha was distracted with all her preparations; and she came up to Him, and said, "Lord, do You not care that my sister has left me to do all the serving alone? Then tell her to help me."** *But the Lord answered and said to her, "Martha, Martha, you are worried and bothered about so many things; but only a few things are necessary, really only one, for Mary has chosen the good part, which shall not be taken away from her."* (Luke 10:38-42 emphasis added)

This is a perfect example of someone who is *doing* and of someone who is *being*! Martha was busy *doing* things for Jesus and Mary was content just *being* in His presence sitting at His feet. Jesus told Martha that Mary had chosen the better part!

Let's pick up the story in John 11 as Jesus was on His way to raise His friend from the dead:

> *Now Bethany was near Jerusalem, about two miles off; and many of the Jews had come to Martha and Mary, to console them concerning their brother. Martha therefore,*

when she heard that Jesus was coming, went to meet Him; but Mary still sat in the house. **Martha therefore said to Jesus, "Lord, if You had been here, my brother would not have died.** "Even now I know that whatever You ask of God, God will give You." Jesus said to her, "Your brother shall rise again." Martha said to Him, "I know that he will rise again in the resurrection on the last day." Jesus said to her, "I am the resurrection and the life; he who believes in Me shall live even if he dies, and everyone who lives and believes in Me shall never die. Do you believe this?" She said to Him, "Yes, Lord; I have believed that You are the Christ, the Son of God, even He who comes into the world." And when she had said this, she went away, and called Mary her sister, saying secretly, "The Teacher is here, and is calling for you." And when she heard it, she arose quickly, and was coming to Him.*

*Now Jesus had not yet come into the village, but was still in the place where Martha met Him. The Jews then who were with her in the house, and consoling her, when they saw that Mary rose up quickly and went out, followed her, supposing that she was going to the tomb to weep there. **Therefore, when Mary came where Jesus was, she saw Him, and fell at His feet, saying to Him, "Lord, if You had been here, my brother would not have died."** When Jesus therefore saw her* *weeping, and the Jews who came with her, also weeping, He was deeply moved in spirit, and was troubled, and said, "Where have you laid him?" They said to Him, "Lord, come and see." Jesus wept.*

There is so much to see in this account! When word came that Jesus was not far away, both of the sisters heard it at the same time, but they responded in different ways. The Word says that Martha went to meet Him, but Mary sat still! This is my first observation: Mary was a worshiper who had a relationship with Jesus! Martha was the busy one. While she had a relationship with Jesus as well, it was based more out of what she did for Him. When you are a worshiper, *one who is intimately acquainted with and having a daily relationship with God exhibited through obedience*, you are not moved by circumstances and situations like others are. I believe Mary sat still because she trusted Jesus and knew everything was going to be fine.

When Martha met Jesus on the road, she said, *"Lord, if you had been here, my brother would not have died!"* Jesus tried to comfort her by saying that Lazarus would live again, and after a few minutes of conversation with Martha, Jesus said something to her that is not recorded but that her actions would suggest. At some point Jesus said to Martha, "Where's Mary? Go get Mary!" How do I know that? Because Martha left Jesus, went to Mary and said, ***"The Teacher is here, and is calling for you."***

It was at that point that Mary got up and went out to meet Jesus. The Bible tells us that Jesus was in exactly the same location He was in when He spoke to Martha. When Mary arrived she said exactly the same words to Jesus that her sister had spoken: *"Lord, if you had been here, my brother would not have died!"* But there was one difference! Her posture!

When Mary arrived at the very spot where Martha had met Jesus, the Word says that **she fell at His feet!** She knelt down in worship! It was *the proper posture before the Savior of the world that then gave opportunity for relationship with Him.* While the words were exactly the same, it was Mary's posture that allowed her words to be heard and that moved Jesus with compassion. The Word says that He wept. Then He responded to Mary by asking, "Where have you laid him?" We know the rest of the story. Lazarus was raised from the dead!

In each of the three accounts we have looked at, you can see that the *proper posture* is an important part of the interaction between the Lord and His people! It is through the *act of worship* that we are able to approach God and be received. It is through the *act of worship* that we demonstrate our willingness to submit to Him in every way!

CHAPTER SIX

Tested and Proven: Worship Lived Out

Once we have shown our willingness to relate to the Lord on His terms, we will find that God sets before us opportunities that will test and prove our commitment to Him. These are not tests designed to destroy us, but rather tests designed to prove us and allow God to prove Himself to us! It is through our knowledge of God and our experiences with Him that we grow in our confidence and trust in Him. These tests are opportunities to grow our faith. No one starts out *full* of faith; our faith grows as it is exercised. The exercising of our faith comes by using it in everyday life experiences. There are, however, what I would call *faith-defining moments of a worshiper*. These are moments in our lives as worshipers when what we profess to believe is put to the test. In every instance, God has allowed these faith-defining moments to come because He knows

His plan for us and He knows we are equipped to handle it. This is how we live out a life of worship that goes beyond posture and beyond words, and each time we respond in faith, obedience and sacrifice is an act of worship before our God!

Those Who Know Their God!

One identifying characteristic of a true worshiper is that they know God. This "knowing" goes beyond simple information about God. In fact the Hebrew word translated as "know" implies perceiving, understanding, and experiencing. It means to take hold of and experience the reality of something or someone. It is not simply to possess knowledge, but the "actualization" of that knowledge. In other words, to know is to make real. It comes from time spent with the Lord in deep communion, in His word, in prayer, in meditation. It is going beyond the words written on the pages of the Bible; it is seeing the Word made flesh.

With that in mind, let's look through the eyes of a worshiper at a familiar verse found in the book of Daniel:

> *". . . but the people who know their God shall be strong, and carry out great exploits."* (Daniel 11:32b NKJV)

> *". . . but the people who know their God shall prove themselves strong and shall stand firm and do exploits [for God]*. (Amplified)

The New American Standard Bible further expands our understanding of this verse:

". . . but the people who know their God will display strength and take action.

There is strength that comes from being a worshiper; there is an undeniable, indisputable strength that comes from experiential knowledge of God and from walking in close, intimate relationship with Him. It is this strength that distinguishes us as the people of God. It is this strength that enables us to do the extraordinary. It is from this strength that we worship with our lives. And from that place of worship we are able to stand during times of testing. As we come to those defining moments of faith, knowing Him brings the strength that enables us to be victorious. It is as we walk in this strength that others see that our God is real, that He is the true and living God and above Him there is no other!

"Now I Know"

In Genesis 22 we see a faith-defining moment for Abraham in the ultimate act of worship. After receiving his promised son, Isaac, the Word says that God tested this worshiper. He instructed Abraham to offer up Isaac as a sacrifice, and in obedience, Abraham took his son up to Mount Moriah and prepared him to be sacrificed. Let's look at what happened:

*Then they came to the place of which God had told him; and Abraham built the altar there, and arranged the wood, and bound his son Isaac, and laid him on the altar on top of the wood. And Abraham stretched out his hand, and took the knife to slay his son. But the angel of the Lord called to him from heaven, and said, "Abraham, Abraham!" And he said, "Here I am." And he said, "Do not stretch out your hand against the lad, and do nothing to him; **for now I know that you fear God**, since you have not withheld your son, your only son, from Me."* (Genesis 22:9-13 emphasis added)

What was this test about and what was the result of the test? I believe we can see the answer in God's response to Abraham's obedience. Right at the point when Abraham was about to sacrifice his son, God stopped him and said to him, *"Lay not thy hand upon the lad, neither do thou anything unto him. For **now I know** that thou fearest God, seeing thou hast not withheld thy son, thine only son, from me."*

What did God mean by this? I believe this was Abraham's final test to show God that he truly and wholeheartedly trusted God. When God said, *"Now I know,"* He was saying, "Abraham, now I know that *you* know that I am God!" Remember, Abraham started out his relationship with God not knowing or fully trusting Him. He had schemed and lied to work through his situations, but not any more! Now many years later he proved to God that he was totally sold out to Him. He had come to know this God as faithful to honor His word. He had seen God move on his behalf over and over again. And I believe it is because he had come to know the heart, the character, the nature of God that Abraham found strength to make Isaac a sacrifice unto the Lord. It was that strength that enabled him to obey God completely.

God showed His pleasure in Abraham by saying to him, "*Because you have not withheld your only son, I will indeed bless you and greatly multiply your seed!*" There are blessings that come from our obedience and sacrifice to God! Even when we don't quite understand what's going on, if we remain faithful, we will eventually understand God's plan and be rewarded for our faithfulness. As we see in the life of Abraham, we too are continually growing in our relationship with God. What is God asking you to surrender to Him in this season as an act of worship? What might you still be holding on to? Every opportunity for growth is an opportunity to worship; every opportunity for surrender is an opportunity to worship. As we grow, may we live in a way, may we worship in a way that God is able to say about us, *"NOW I KNOW!"*

Some years ago I faced a faith-defining moment, one of many that I have had over the course of my life. I was tested through the ministry, through individuals who I trusted and believed had my best interest at heart. I must admit that I was ready to walk away from it all. But I knew what the Lord had spoken to me. And I had learned over a lifetime of relationship with Him that what He promised He was not only able to perform, but He would perform! I knew the challenges were only tests designed to strengthen and better prepare me for the call on my life. It was during that time I penned these words:

Sometimes it's hard to see what lies before
    me;
The future, once so bright, seems so unclear.
My mind says to worry,
But my heart says wait on You.
You will see me through this
Give me grace to do this
Lovingly, You'll guide me all the way.
You will see me through this
Give me grace to do this
With faith in You, I'll go
For in my heart I know
You will see me through this too.
The tests and trials want to confound me
In hope I'll walk away from You
But Your Word says that all things
Will work out for my good.
You will see me through this
Give me grace to do this
Lovingly, You'll guide me all the way.
You will see me through this
Give me grace to do this
With faith in You, I'll go
For in my heart I know
You will see me through this too.

The life of a worshiper is not without tests, nor is without the pressure that comes with living in a sinful world. It is God's grace that strengthens us and helps us to walk in victory even in our most challenging times! For the worshiper, every test is preparing us to one day rule and reign with Jesus! It is important that we not lose this perspective.

They Knew Their God

Having now broadened our definition of a worshiper - *one who is intimately acquainted with and has a daily relationship with God exhibited through obedience* - it is easy for us to identify worshipers throughout the Scriptures in order to learn from them. We see many worshipers who were tested and proven as they lived a life of worship before God. Four such men are found in the book of Daniel.

Daniel, Hananiah, Mishael, and Azariah were worshipers who faced many *faith-defining moments*. These young men had been taken into captivity by the Babylonians during the time that Jerusalem was under siege. The plan of the Babylonians was to indoctrinate them into the ways of the Chaldeans. In the first chapter of Daniel, we can see what their plan was for these young men:

Then the king ordered Ashpenaz, the chief of his officials, to bring in some of the sons of Israel, including some of the royal family and of the nobles, youths in whom was no defect, who were good-looking, showing intelligence in every branch of wisdom, endowed with understanding, and discerning knowledge, and who had ability for serving in the king's court; and he ordered him to teach them the literature and language of the Chaldeans. And the king appointed for them a daily ration from the king's choice food and from the wine which he drank, and appointed that they should be educated three years, at the end of which they were to enter the king's personal service. Now among them from the sons of Judah were Daniel, Hananiah, Mishael and Azariah. Then the commander of the officials assigned new names to them; and to Daniel he assigned the name Belteshazzar, to Hananiah Shadrach, to Mishael Meshach, and to Azariah Abed-nego. (Daniel 1:3-7)

Notice the process by which the Babylonians attempted to change these young men. They wanted to change their names, change their diet, and change their language. They understood that to change a people and their culture it is necessary to remove everything that is familiar to them and replace it with something else. If they could change their language, change their names, and change their diet they would be well on their way to creating a new culture and a very different future for them. The Babylonians knew that if they were going to benefit from having these young men in their possession, they would have to change them! Their plan was to strip them of their

Godly heritage by removing from them any memory of their past.

In today's society we see the same type of process happening in our school systems, in our colleges and universities and, yes, in many of our churches! We have a generation of young people who are being taught new philosophies and new ways of thinking. Our children find themselves under the influence of the secularist and humanist, who subtly infuse their minds with ideas that are most often opposed to the Word of God and do not affirm who they are created to be in Christ. Many of our children have become lost because we have not continued to teach and share the Word of God in our every day lives. This is why it is so important today for us to continue to share with our children and the future generations the Word of God, our faith and the lifestyle of being a worshiper!

God knew this would happen to His people; that is why He told the children of Israel to speak of Him and His goodness daily to one another and to teach their children and their children's children! He commanded them saying:

> *And these words, which I am commanding you today, shall be on your heart; and you shall teach them diligently to your sons and shall talk of them when you sit in your house and when you walk by the way and when you lie down and when you rise up. And you shall bind them as a sign on your hand and they shall be as frontals on your forehead.*

And you shall write them on the doorposts of your house and on your gates. (Deuteronomy 6:6-9)

God knew that it was important to get the word in them and teach them to have a relationship with Him from an early age. When they faced challenges as these four young men faced in Babylon, they would know Him, know themselves, and be strong enough to take a stand against anything ungodly.

A Purposeful Heart

Because these young men knew their God and knew who they were in their God, they were able to take a stand. I believe that they did not take on the Babylonian names given to them; their Hebrew names were a reminder of who God had called them to *be.* Understand that Babylon represents a world system that tries to strip us of our God-given, God-defined identity. These men, Daniel (God is My Judge), Hananiah (Gift of the Lord), Mishael (Who is Asked For) and Azariah (He That Hears the Lord) maintained their identity by withstanding the system intent on changing them. When the young men were offered food from the king's table, Daniel spoke up on their behalf and said they would not eat the food.

But Daniel purposed in his heart that he would not defile himself with the portion of the king's delicacies, nor with the wine which he drank; therefore he requested of the chief

*of the eunuchs that he might not defile himself.
Now God had brought Daniel into the favor
and goodwill of the chief of the eunuchs.
And the chief of the eunuchs said to Daniel,
"I fear my lord the king, who has appointed
your food and drink. For why should he see
your faces looking worse than the young men
who are your age? Then you would endanger
my head before the king." So Daniel said to
the steward whom the chief of the eunuchs
had set over Daniel, Hananiah, Mishael, and
Azariah, "Please test your servants for ten
days, and let them give us vegetables to eat
and water to drink. Then let our appearance
be examined before you, and the appearance
of the young men who eat the portion of the
king's delicacies; and as you see fit, so deal
with your servants."* (Daniel 1:8-13 NKJV
emphasis added)

Daniel had strong convictions about his relationship with God. The Word says that *"he purposed
in his heart that he would not defile himself."* As
worshipers it is important to know our heart. Many
years ago while doing a study on the heart as it
relates to worship, I came across a definition in the
book *The Making of a Leader* by Frank Damazio that
helped me to understand what it truly means to give
one's heart to the Lord. DaMazio's definition comes
from the Greek word for heart, "kardia." It refers to
the thoughts, desires, passions, appetites, affections,
purposes and endeavors of a person. True worshipers

allow the Holy Spirit to search their hearts and do whatever is necessary to align every thought, desire, passion, appetite, affection, purpose and endeavor with heart of the Father. When Jesus is truly the Lord in our lives, He is the One who sits on the throne of our hearts, and as Lord, He is the One we allow to rule and reign over every area of our hearts.

After years of singing about the heart, I realized in my own life that I had not completely understood what it meant to give my heart to the Lord. As I looked over my life, I could see inconsistencies in my walk with the Lord. When I cried out to Him to help me understand why that was and to help me change, He began to show me the areas of my heart that were not yielded to Him. It was during that moment of personal reflection and worship that the Lord gave me the words to a song that is my personal response to His love for me. You see, when we reflect on all the Lord has done to bring us into that love relationship with Him, when we reflect on all He has done to save us, on the magnitude of His love for us and His grace toward us, our only response is to give our hearts completely to Him; nothing short of that will do. Our only response is to declare "My Heart is Your Throne."

> How can I ever pay
> The debt I owe
> When I know the price You paid to save my
>   soul?
> The more You ask, the more I'll give;
> I'll serve You, Lord, each day I live

My heart is Your throne.
Heaven gave its greatest gift
When You came down
To redeem me from my sin,
You gave Your life
And now You live forevermore
Within my heart;
You are my Lord
My heart is Your throne.
I give You my heart;
Forever it shall be
A place where You can rule and reign.
Until I see Your face
In our eternal home
My heart is Your throne
King of Kings; Lord of all;
The El-Shaddai,
Mighty God; the Great I Am —
That's Who You are.
I bow my knee with heart in hand;
Your every Word is my command.
My heart is Your throne
I give You my heart;
Forever it shall be
A place where You can rule and reign.
Until I see Your face
In our eternal home
My heart is Your throne.

When I read that Daniel "purposed in his heart,"
I believe that every one of these areas of his heart
– his thoughts, desires, passions, appetite, affections,

purposes and endeavors — were yielded to God. Daniel was able to yield his whole heart because he knew his God and that gave him and his young companions the strength and the courage to stand! As worshipers, we will be faced many times with opportunities to compromise our faith. But just like Daniel, we must purpose in our heart to stand for righteousness and holiness. It is a decision that is best made *before* we find ourselves faced with the situation. Only then can we be sure to stand in that moment!

Daniel knew that much of the food from the king's table had been offered to idols. He chose to take a risk by refusing to eat the food, and God honored him by giving him favor with the prince of the eunuchs, who agreed to let them eat only vegetables and drink only water for ten days. At the end of the ten days when he compared them to the other young men who had eaten from the king's table, he found Daniel, Hananiah, Mishael, and Azariah's appearance healthier than the other young men. God had honored the stand that these young men took as an act of worship, and when they were finally presented to the king, God granted them favor with the king also!

> *And as for these four youths, God gave them knowledge and intelligence in every branch of literature and wisdom; Daniel even understood all kinds of visions and dreams. Then at the end of the days which the king had specified for presenting them, the commander of the officials presented them before Nebuchadnezzar. And the king talked with*

*them, and out of them all not one was found
like Daniel, Hananiah, Mishael and Azariah;
so they entered the king's personal service.
And as for every matter of wisdom and understanding about which the king consulted
them, he found them ten times better than all
the magicians and conjurers who were in all
his realm. And Daniel continued until the first
year of Cyrus the king.* (Daniel 1:17-21)

Great Exploits

Soon Daniel was faced with another test, another
faith-defining moment. This time it was the king who
would put the test before him. In the second chapter
of Daniel, King Nebuchadnezzar had had a dream
that troubled him. He looked to the Chaldean magicians, enchanters, sorcerers to interpret the dream for
him.

*And the king said to them, "I had a dream,
and my spirit is anxious to understand the
dream." Then the Chaldeans spoke to the king
in Aramaic: "O king, live forever! Tell the
dream to your servants, and we will declare
the interpretation." The king answered and
said to the Chaldeans, "The command from
me is firm: if you do not make known to me
the dream and its interpretation, you will be
torn limb from limb, and your houses will be
made a rubbish heap. "But if you declare the
dream and its interpretation, you will receive*

from me gifts and a reward and great honor;
therefore declare to me the dream and its
interpretation." (Daniel 2:3-6)

The king's request seemed to be impossible, and
the Chaldeans response showed that they believed no
one was capable of doing such a thing.

The Chaldeans answered the king and said,
"There is not a man on earth who could
declare the matter for the king, inasmuch
as no great king or ruler has ever asked
anything like this of any magician, conjurer
or Chaldean. "Moreover, the thing which the
king demands is difficult, and there is no one
else who could declare it to the king except
gods, whose dwelling place is not with mortal
flesh." (Daniel 2:10-11)

King Nebuchadnezzar was enraged by their
response and commanded that all of them, including
Daniel, Hananiah, Mishael and Azariah, be put to
death! Once Daniel got word of this, he petitioned
the king for time to show him the interpretation of his
dream. The king agreed. Daniel immediately went to
Hananiah, Mishael, and Azariah and together they
sought the Lord.

Then Daniel went to his house and informed
his friends, Hananiah, Mishael and Azariah,
about the matter, in order that they might
request compassion from the God of heaven

concerning this mystery, so that Daniel and his friends might not be destroyed with the rest of the wise men of Babylon. Then the mystery was revealed to Daniel in a night vision. Then Daniel blessed the God of heaven; (Daniel 2:17-19)

Could it be that because these men were worshipers and knew their God, they knew they could petition Him and expect Him to respond? I believe because these young men were worshipers God answered their request. He gave Daniel the dream and its interpretation! And the first thing Daniel did was to worship God for giving him the answer. He then approached the man given the responsibility to execute them and told him he had the answer the king was looking for! Neither King Nebuchadnezzar nor the Chaldeans really knew the relationship Daniel and his friends had with their God, but they were about to find out!

Daniel was brought before the Nebuchadnezzar and questioned as to whether he truly had the interpretation. The Bible says:

*Daniel answered before the king and said, "As for the mystery about which the king has inquired, neither wise men, conjurers, magicians, nor diviners are able to declare it to the king. "**However, there is a God in heaven who reveals mysteries,** and He has made known to King Nebuchadnezzar what will take place in the latter days. This was your dream and the visions in your mind while* *on your bed. "As for you, O king, while on your bed your thoughts turned to what would take place in the future; and He who reveals mysteries has made known to you what will take place."* **But as for me, this mystery has not been revealed to me for any wisdom residing in me more than in any other living man, but for the purpose of making the interpretation known to the king, and that you may understand the thoughts of your mind.** (Daniel 2:27-30 emphasis added)

Notice that Daniel was careful to give all the credit and glory to God! He then proceeded to tell Nebuchadnezzar the dream and its interpretation. We rarely think of this as an "exploit" but it was! A worshiper, one intimately acquainted with and having a daily relationship with God, exhibited by his obedience, found the strength to stand and as a result was able to do what no one else in Babylon had been able to do. In the end, we see how the king honored Daniel.

"Then King Nebuchadnezzar fell on his face and did homage to Daniel, and gave orders to present to him an offering and fragrant incense. The king answered Daniel and said, "Surely your God is a God of gods and a Lord of kings and a revealer of mysteries, since you have been able to reveal this mystery." Then the king promoted Daniel and gave him many great gifts, and he made him ruler over the

whole province of Babylon and chief prefect over all the wise men of Babylon. And Daniel made request of the king, and he appointed Shadrach, Meshach and Abed-nego over the administration of the province of Babylon, while Daniel was at the king's court." (Daniel 2:46-49)

The king was so impressed with Daniel that he promoted him. Daniel, in turn, asked that his friends be promoted as well and they were. We serve the Only God! There is nothing hidden to Him! He sees all and knows all! Just as we see with Daniel, our God is able to reveal secrets to those who are worshipers!

An Invitation to Compromise

Hananiah, Mishael and Azariah were promoted at the request of their friend, Daniel. As a result of another decree by King Nebuchadnezzar, they were faced with their own test. Nebuchadnezzar had erected a statute in his own image. He then invited all of the leaders and employees under his rule to attend the dedication of the statue. This invitation included Hananiah, Mishael and Azariah. They, along with the other leaders, were instructed that at the time they heard the music play, they were to bow down and worship the idol. Anyone who did not do so would face death in the fiery furnace.

When the music began to play, everyone bowed down — everyone except Hananiah, Mishael and Azariah. Some of the Chaldeans went to the king to report, "The Jews you appointed over the affairs of the providence of Babylon did not obey you!"

"For this reason at that time certain Chaldeans came forward and brought charges against the Jews. They responded and said to Nebuchadnezzar the king: "O king, live forever! "You yourself, O king, have made a decree that every man who hears the sound of the horn, flute, lyre, trigon, psaltery, and bagpipe, and all kinds of music, is to fall down and worship the golden image. "But whoever does not fall down and worship shall be cast into the midst of a furnace of blazing fire. "There are certain Jews whom you have appointed over the administration of the province of Babylon, namely Shadrach, Meshach and Abed-nego. These men, O king, have disregarded you; they do not serve your gods or worship the golden image which you have set up." (Daniel 3:8-12 emphasis added)

When Nebuchadnezzar heard that they had not bowed down, he was infuriated. He demanded that they be brought to him and he presented them with another opportunity to spare their lives. He offered to have the music played again, and if they bowed down and worshiped the idol everything would be fine. But if they refused to bow down, certain death. This was the response of these three worshipers:

*Shadrach, Meshach and Abed-nego answered
and said to the king, "O Nebuchadnezzar, we
do not need to give you an answer concerning
this matter. "If it be so, our God whom we
serve is able to deliver us from the furnace
of blazing fire; and He will deliver us out of
your hand, O king. "But even if He does not,
let it be known to you, O king, that we are
not going to serve your gods or worship the
golden image that you have set up." (*Daniel
3:16-18 emphasis added)

This was another faith-defining moment for these
three worshipers! They made it absolutely clear that
they would not compromise; they would not bow! As
worshipers they were confident in their God and His
ability to keep them! Now the king was incensed by
their response!

*Then Nebuchadnezzar was filled with wrath,
and his facial expression was altered toward
Shadrach, Meshach and Abed-nego. He
answered by giving orders to heat the furnace
seven times more than it was usually heated.
And he commanded certain valiant warriors
who were in his army to tie up Shadrach,
Meshach and Abed-nego, in order to cast
them into the furnace of blazing fire. (*Daniel
3:19-21)

At this point it looked like these men would surely
die for their beliefs. They were tied up and thrown

into the fiery furnace and that's when the miracle happened! These young men, these worshipers were now joined in the fire by the One they worship! Nebuchadnezzar was astonished by what he saw and called others to come and look! What they saw was beyond belief: the young men who had been tied up and thrown into the fire, were now walking around free and unharmed in the midst of the fire!

Our faith will be tested and we may even be asked to bow and pay homage to an "idol" of some kind. It may not be a statue as it was in the case of these Hananiah, Mishael and Azariah, but every day we are faced with choices that test what we truly believe. Every time we choose God over everything else is an act of worship. And that choice may cost us. But the prophet Isaiah tells us that when we find ourselves situations that threaten our very lives, we can be assured that God is with us, just as He was with the three Hebrew boys:

> *"When you pass through the waters, I will be*
> *   with you;*
> *And through the rivers, they will not overflow*
> *   you.*
> *When you walk through the fire, you will not*
> *   be scorched,*
> *Nor will the flame burn you.* (Isaiah 43:2)

Nebuchadnezzar eventually called these three worshipers of the true God to come out of fiery furnace and when they did, he noticed that not only was not a hair on their heads singed, but they didn't even smell of smoke! The king and all the people stood in amazement! God had honored these young men's stand and proved Himself for all to see. Nebuchadnezzar then made another decree that anyone who spoke against the God of Hananiah, Mishael and Azariah would be put to death!

What lessons can we learn about worship from the lives of these Hebrew young men? I believe there are many. We see in them a life that is given over to the Lord. They knew their God and every choice they made reflected that knowledge, and each choice they made to honor the true and living God was an act of worship. And so it is with us. Each time we choose to walk in integrity, to stand for righteousness, to walk in holiness, to stand up against the world system that seeks to mold us into its image, to stand on every promise of God despite the challenges is an act of worship. Each time we give of our substance and of ourselves is an act of worship. Each time we strive for excellence in all we do is an act of worship. It's not in our song; it is in each choice we make that we declare Jesus is Lord!

Hananiah, Mishael and Azariah passed their test and were promoted to even greater roles of influence. As I stated earlier, God does not test us to destroy us, but rather to make us! As worshipers, we must come to expect times when we will be tested. But remember that those who *know* their God are strong and are able to stand. In every case, God honors and protects those who are intimately acquainted with and have as daily relationship with Him as exhibited through their obedience to His word. He honors His worshipers!

CHAPTER SEVEN

JESUS! The Perfect Worshipper!

We established in the first chapter that Adam was created *as* a worshiper. He, created in the image of the Father, was designed to *be intimately acquainted with and have a daily relationship with God exhibited through obedience.* By his disobedience, he abdicated his role, requiring that there be a second Adam. That second Adam was JESUS! If Adam was the first model of a worshiper, it is only fitting that we look at the One Who came to re-establish that worship relationship for all of us! We can look down through the ages at many who were used by God in their generation. We can look at many who worshiped God, but there is only One Perfect Worshiper: JESUS! He is the model we *must* follow!

Jesus perfectly exemplified the life Adam was created to live, a life that was one with the Father; a life that was lived in total dependence on the Father. Jesus always walked in the authority the Father had given and had dominion over all of creation, over all of nature, even over the winds and waves. His was a life that never lost sight of purpose and destiny. He lived a life of unwavering faith. In all He did, He perfectly reflected the image of our Father. It was out of His life of intimacy and daily relationship with the Father that Jesus destroyed the works of the devil. It was His obedience unto death – the ultimate sacrifice — that allows us to be His family of worshipers.

To Do the Will of the Father

There is very little said in the Bible about Jesus' childhood. But it does tell us, "Jesus increased in wisdom and stature and in *favor with God* and man." Even as a child, Jesus was focused on pleasing His Father, doing His will, and walking out the purpose for which He had been born. Luke writes:

> *And the Child grew and became strong in spirit, filled with wisdom; and the grace of God was upon Him. His parents went to Jerusalem every year at the Feast of the Passover. **And when He was twelve years old, they went up to Jerusalem according to the custom of the feast.** When they had finished the days, as they returned, the Boy Jesus lingered behind in Jerusalem. And Joseph and His mother did not know it; but supposing Him to have been in the company, they went*

a day's journey, and sought Him among their relatives and acquaintances. So when they did not find Him, they returned to Jerusalem, seeking Him. **Now so it was that after three days they found Him in the temple, sitting in the midst of the teachers, both listening to them and asking them questions. And all who heard Him were astonished at His understanding and answers. So when they saw Him, they were amazed; and His mother said to Him, "Son, why have You done this to us? Look, Your father and I have sought You anxiously." And He said to them, "Why did you seek Me? Did you not know that I must be about My Father's business?"** *But they did not understand the statement which He spoke to them.*

Then He went down with them and came to Nazareth, and was subject to them, but His mother kept all these things in her heart. **And Jesus increased in wisdom and stature, and in favor with God and men.** (Luke 2:40-52 NKJV emphasis added)

As a young boy, Jesus sought to do the will of the Father. He knew He had been born with a specific purpose and He was intent on fulfilling it. He declared to His parents, "I *must be about My Father's business,"* or more accurately translated *"I must be about the things of My Father."* This is important because while it is His death on the cross that paid the price for our sins, it is the way He lived His entire life that qualified Him to be the perfect worshiper and the perfect sacrifice! Jesus did not just come to die for us, but to live a life before men that would model the life of a worshiper. He lived the life that would be available to every man who would believe on Him after His death and resurrection.

We see Jesus focused always on the purposes of God, totally consumed by the will of the Father. He said, *"My food is to do the will of Him Who sent me and to finish it."* (John 4:34)

> *". . . I do not seek my own will but the will of the father who sent Me."* (John 5:30)
>
> *"I have come down from heaven, not to do My own will, but the will of Him who sent Me."* (John 6:38)

Jesus maintained a place of discipline as He walked the earth. During the three and one half years of His public ministry, He never once allowed the people to deter Him from His purpose. There were many times that He was asked to establish His kingdom. There were many times the people wanted to make Him king and some even tried to force His hand. But He remained focused on His ultimate goal: salvation and restoration of worshipers by way of the cross. Jesus never gave in to public opinion, whether it was positive or negative. Unlike Adam who listened to the voice of another and sought independence from God, Jesus listened for and listened to one voice only– the voice of the Father. He did not seek to do anything outside the will of God. He remained dependent on

His Father and all He did issued forth from that place on dependence.

From the Place of Being

As we have sought to rethink our definition of a worshiper; we have established a distinction between the state of being a worshiper and the acts or expression of worship. We have concluded that it is from the state of being that all acts of worship must flow. This is equally true of Jesus.

> *"Now it came about when all the people were baptized, that Jesus also was baptized, and while He was praying, heaven was opened, and the Holy Spirit descended upon Him in bodily form like a dove, and a voice came out of heaven, **"Thou art My beloved Son, in Thee I am well-pleased."** And when He began His ministry, Jesus Himself was about thirty years of age..." Luke 3:21-23*

This is the beginning of Jesus' public ministry. As He was being baptized, the Father spoke from heaven declaring His delight in His Son. Scripture does not tell us that Jesus had done anything necessarily spectacular up to this point. We have no record of a miracle and His death and resurrection are three and a half years away. He hasn't *done* anything, yet the Father declared that He was well-pleased with His Son. *The MESSAGE: The Bible in Contemporary Language* says it this way, "*You are my Son, chosen and marked by my love, pride of my life."* The New Living Translation says *"You are my dearly loved Son, and you bring me great joy!"* God's pleasure did not stem from what Jesus *did* but who He *was!* It stemmed from the relationship Jesus had with His Father. God knew that from that state of being a worshiper, Jesus would perfectly walk out in the natural that which He had purposed before the foundations of the world were laid. That act of worship was a natural result of His relationship with God.

Throughout His life, Jesus declared *Who* He was. He did not say, "I speak truth" rather "I AM the Truth." He did not proclaim, "I will show you the way" but "I AM the Way." He did not simply say, "I will give you life" but "I Am the Life." Nor did He promise "I will resurrect you some day" but "I Am the Resurrection." He announced "I AM!" All the things He *did* sprang forth from of His *being.*

Intimately Acquainted

Jesus showed us that the life of a worshiper is a life of continual communion and communication with the Father. It was this type of daily communion with God that Adam had once experienced in the Garden. Adam had been created to walk in continual communion with God, to live a life of fellowship and friendship with Him. Jesus exemplified this aspect of a worshiper's life through a life of prayer! Luke shares with us, more than any other writer, the frequency and fervency of Jesus' life of prayer.

*"But He Himself would often slip away to
the wilderness and pray. . ." (Luke 5:16)*

*"And it came about that while He was
praying alone. . ."* (Luke 9:18)

*"Now it came to pass, as He was praying
in a certain place. . ."* (Luke 11:1)

Every decision Jesus made was in direct align-
ment with His Father. We read that it was only after
a night of prayer that He chose the twelve that would
follow Him. He was able to walk in such harmony
and agreement with the Father because He lived a
life of prayer.

***And it was at this time that He went off to
the mountain to pray, and He spent the
whole night in prayer to God.*** *And when day
came, He called His disciples to Him; and
chose twelve of them, whom He also named
as apostles: Simon, whom He also named
Peter, and Andrew his brother; and James
and John; and Philip and Bartholomew;
and Matthew and Thomas; James the son
of Alphaeus, and Simon who was called the
Zealot; Judas the son of James, and Judas
Iscariot, who became a traitor.* (Luke 6:12-
17 emphasis added)

Jesus regularly stole away to be alone with God,
to spend time in His presence, to hear His heart and
to know His mind. He emerged from those times of

prayer empowered to carry out, by faith, the will of God.

> ***"Jesus therefore answered and was saying to them, "Truly, truly, I say to you, the Son can do nothing of Himself, unless it is something He sees the Father doing; for whatever the Father does, these things the Son also does in like manner.*** *"For the Father loves the Son, and shows Him all things that He Himself is doing; and greater works than these will He show Him, that you may marvel."* (John 5:19 emphasis added)

It was through communion and fellowship with the Father that Jesus first saw what God desired to manifest in the earth and He heard the words the Father desired to speak into the lives of men and women. It was because of His communion with God that Jesus was then able to do what He had seen and speak what He had heard. It was through this continual exchange that Jesus remained totally submitted to God's will.

Dominion, Authority and Power

Following His baptism, Jesus was "led" into the wilderness and there He was tested by the devil. It was satan's attempt to stop Jesus as he had stopped Adam. It was the enemy's attempt to sever the relationship between God and His Worshiper.

"And Jesus, full of the Holy Spirit, returned from the Jordan and was led about by the Spirit in the wilderness for forty days, being tempted by the devil. And He ate nothing during those days; and when they had ended, He became hungry. **And the devil said to Him, "If You are the Son of God, tell this stone to become bread."** *And Jesus answered him, "It is written, 'Man shall not live on bread alone.'" And he led Him up and showed Him all the kingdoms of the world in a moment of time.* **And the devil said to Him, "I will give You all this domain and its glory; for it has been handed over to me, and I give it to whomever I wish. "Therefore if You worship before me, it shall all be Yours."** *And Jesus answered and said to him, "It is written, 'You shall worship the Lord your God and serve Him only.'" And he led Him to Jerusalem and had Him stand on the pinnacle of the temple, and said to Him, "If You are the Son of God, throw Yourself down from here;* **for it is written, 'He will give His angels charge concerning You to guard You,' and, 'On their hands they will bear You up, Lest You strike Your foot against a stone.'"** *And Jesus answered and said to him, "It is said, 'You shall not put the Lord your God to the test.'" And when the devil had finished every temptation, he departed from Him until an opportune time."* (Luke 4:1-13 emphasis added)

117

Jesus was tempted in the same areas in which every person is tempted. He was tempted in the same way that Adam had been: through the lust of the flesh, the lust of the eye, and the pride of life as found in 1 John 2:15-17. This is what it says:

Love not the world, neither the things that are in the world. If any man love the world, the love of the Father is not in him. **For all that is in the world, the lust of the flesh and the lust of the eyes and the vain glory of life, is not of the Father, but is of the world.** *And the world passeth away, and the lust thereof: but he that doeth the will of God abideth for ever.* (emphasis added)

The enemy knew if he could get Jesus to do one thing outside of the will of the Father, it would be over! All would be forfeited! All would be lost! Thank God, Jesus knew what satan was trying to do. Jesus knew what weighed in the balance and did not allow Himself to be drawn into a competition or debate. Jesus gained victory over satan by speaking the Word of God and by keeping His focus on the Father! This was the first of many tests that Jesus would face on His way to the cross! For once the enemy knew Who Jesus was, he was out to stop Him any way he could.

By defeating the enemy at every turn, Jesus demonstrated the life of a worshiper. We don't often think of it that way. Adam had been given authority and dominion; walking in that authority and dominion is an act of worship. Each time Jesus used the authority given Him, each time He took dominion was an act of worship. Each time He came up against sickness and disease, each time He came up against false religion, lies and deception, He demonstrated the power and authority man was to have from the very beginning. Even calming the sea and the wind by simply speaking to them was an act of worship. Jesus declared that He had come to destroy the works of the devil. He came to destroy that which hindered us from being the worshipers God had designed us to be; He came to return authority and dominion to man. Jesus modeled for us that as a worshiper we can withstand the attacks of the enemy and be victorious! He eventually gave His life so that His victory would become ours!

In His Image

The first Adam was to be a reflection of God's glory in the earth; he was created to be the mirror image of God! The authority, dominion and creative ability were available to Adam so that he could reflect His creator, His Father. When Adam sinned that image was marred and he came "short of the glory." The second Adam came to restore that image, to restore the glory.

Jesus lived His life to glorify His Father. Everything He did was with that thought in mind! He reflected God's goodness, God's mercy, God's grace, God's compassion, God's patience, and God's love for mankind! Each time anyone looked at Jesus they were able to see the Father.

> *"Philip said to Him, "Lord, show us the Father, and it is enough for us." Jesus said to him, "Have I been so long with you, and yet you have not come to know Me, Philip?* **He who has seen Me has seen the Father;** *how do you say, 'Show us the Father'? "Do you not believe that I am in the Father, and the Father is in Me? The words that I say to you I do not speak on My own initiative, but the Father abiding in Me does His works."* (John 14:8-11)

We see throughout the Word of God that Jesus did precisely what man had been created to do:

> *"And the Word became flesh, and dwelt among us, and we beheld His glory,* **glory as of the only begotten from the Father,** *full of grace and truth." John 1:14*
>
> **"And He [Jesus] is the image of the invisible God, the first-born of all creation."** *Col 1:15*
>
> **"For in Him all the fulness of Deity dwells in bodily form,** *and in Him you have been made complete, and He is the head over all rule and authority;" Col 2:9-11*
>
> **"And He is the radiance of His glory and the exact representation of His nature,** *and upholds all things by the word of His power.*

When He had made purification of sins, He sat down at the right hand of the Majesty on high;" Hebrews 1:3

Not only did Jesus reflect the Father as Adam had been created to do, through His finished work on the cross and the process of sanctification, we too can reflect that same image.

Obedience that Leads to Sacrifice

Jesus showed us that the life of a worshiper is a life of obedience to the Father. Obedience even unto death! Paul writes in the book of Philippians, reminding us that if we are to truly follow in the footsteps of our Lord, we must be obedient even as He was obedient!

*Have this mind in you, which was also in Christ Jesus: who, existing in the form of God, counted not the being on an equality with God a thing to be grasped, but emptied himself, taking the form of a servant, being made in the likeness of men; and **being found in fashion as a man, he humbled himself, becoming obedient even unto death, yea, the death of the cross.** Wherefore also God highly exalted him, and gave unto him the name which is above every name; that in the name of Jesus every knee should bow, of things in heaven and things on earth and things under the earth, and that every tongue* *should confess that Jesus Christ is Lord, to the glory of God the Father.*

Jesus' obedience led to sacrifice, the sacrifice of His very life so that we might live as worshipers. The writer of Hebrews tells us that even though He was a Son, He learned obedience from the things that He suffered. He set before us the example of one totally surrendered to the will of the Father, able to endure even the cross so that God would be glorified. The end result was that He also was glorified. As we learn to walk in obedience, we shall be glorified together with Him. Our worship will reflect His glory for all to see.

Jesus Christ became the first of many sons, the first of many worshipers, and He set before us the *perfect* model of worship — beyond a song, beyond a dance, beyond the words of love and adoration that we offer up to the Father. Our worship is a life that perfectly reflects the love, light and life of the Father. It is a life lived by walking in the authority and dominion God has given us. It is a life that walks out Kingdom purposes, establishing God's kingdom on earth as it is in heaven; it is a life of kingdom influence, kingdom impact with kingdom results. It is a life lived from the "secret place." It is a life of faith, obedience and sacrifice. It is a deep, intimate relationship with the Father that allows us to know His heart and mind. It is a life that allows others to see God every time they look at us. It is a life lived in the confidence of knowing who we are called to *be* – Worshipers by Design!

About the Author

John W. Stevenson is the founder and president of Heirs International Ministries, Heirs Media Group where he serves as President and CEO, and Heirs Covenant Church of Cincinnati, located in West Chester, Ohio just north of Cincinnati where he serves as senior pastor.

With over 30 years of ministry experience, John has served in numerous ministries as pastor, associate pastor, prophet, teacher, evangelist, worship leader, and chief musician. John is also a songwriter, recording artist and the author of *Nothing But the Truth: A Lifestyle of Christian Integrity* and *The Second Flood: The Discipline of Worship.*

As a music producer, John has recorded 11 projects. John's songs have been recorded by various ministries and artist including Darwin Hobbs (EMIGospel), Bishop Joseph Garlington, David and Nicole Binion, Lenny LeBlanc for Integrity Music, Bishop Paul Morton and Full Gospel Baptist Church and His songs are sung in churches and conferences all over the world.

John was on the faculty and taught at the International Worship Institute and has also taught at the Caribbean Worship Institute in Curacao. He has also worked with and led worship for Global Harvest Ministry, a prayer and intercession ministry headed by C. Peter Wagner of Fuller Theological Seminary and for The Call, headed by Lou Engle. John has ministered with individuals such as Bishop Eddie Long in Atlanta, GA., Dr. Bill Hamon of Christian International, the late Dr. Edwin Louis Cole of Christian Men's Network, Dr. Myles Munroe, worship leaders Ron Kenoly, Kent Henry, Marty Nystrom, William Murphy III, and Lamar Boschman. John's ministry and service in the Body of Christ is well respected, diverse and crosses racial and denominational lines.

John travels the United States and abroad ministering throughout the Body of Christ in an apostolic/prophetic office to church leaders and in churches and conferences. John is a much sought after worshiper leader for conferences. John is a member of Reconciliation! Ministries International, an organization founded by Bishop Joseph Garlington, who also serves as John's pastor.

John has a desire and passion to see the Body of Christ walk in Kingdom influence, Kingdom impact with Kingdom results. John is married to the lovely Marissa Stevenson, and they are the parents of four sons, one daughter and grandparents of one grandson.

If you are interesting in having John minister in your area, or if you would like to order other products, you may contact John at:
Heirs International Ministries
P.O. Box 542
West Chester, Ohio 45071-0542
(513) 942-7242
Fax: (513) 942-4025
Or
Visit our website:
www.heirsintlministries.com

God Speaks:
Words for the Journey from the Father's Heart
By
Deborah A. Gaston

In *God Speaks: Words for the Journey from the Heart of the Father,* author Deborah A. Gaston shares with the reader the "God-side" of dialogues with the heavenly Father. This compilation of words of encouragement, instruction, healing and hope allow you to know in an even greater measure the love that God has for all His children, and will strengthen you as you walk through the process that leads to perfection in Christ. Through these words you will better understand that all things do indeed work together for good to them that love the Lord. These words from the Father's heart will inspire you to know Him in a deeper way.

Deborah A. Gaston has a passion for God's presence and a deep love for His word. A worship leader, teacher, minister of God's word and a prophetic voice in the body of Christ, Deborah has traveled in the United States and abroad, sharing the love of God through worship and the word. A retired Cincinnati Public School teacher, Deborah now serves as the pastor of Music Worship and Arts at the Heirs Covenant Church of Cincinnati.

Available at
www.xulonpress.com
and
www.amazon.com